NANCY BUSH

FOLK SOCKS

THE HISTORY & TECHNIQUES OF HANDKNITTED FOOTWEAR

INTERWEAVE PRESS

LOVELAND, COLORADO

Acknowledgements for historic photographs:
Aberdeen University Library 30; Estonian National Museum 6, 42, 43, 103; Glasgow Museums and Art Galleries—The Burrell Collection 25, 85; Kultren, Lund, Sweden 34, 35, 73; McCormick Collection—Courtesy, Museum of Fine Arts, Boston 16; Museum of London 10; National Museum of Lithuania 105; Nordeska Museet, Stockholm 91; Royal Armory (Livrustkammaren), Stockholm 15; National Museum of Scotland 27, 106; Royal Ontario Museum 45, 81, 114; Staatliche Museen zu Berlin 99; Sutcliff Gallery, Whitby, England 18; Textile Museum, Washington, D.C. 13, 78; Collection of Lizbeth Upitis 41, 93; Vesterheim Norwegian-American Museum, Decorah, IA 38, 76; Vindolanda Trust, Chesterholm Museum 8; Welsh Folk Museum 20, 21, 22, 23; Yale University Art Gallery—Dura Europos Archive 12

Design, Susan Wasinger, Signorella Graphic Arts
Photography, Joe Coca
Illustration, Susan Strawn
Photo styling, Judith Durant
Back cover photo, Joe Gardner
Needlepoint miniature carpet on page 77, Frank M. Cooper

© 1994, Nancy Bush
Photography (except as noted above) © 1994, Interweave Press LLC

Interweave Press LLC
201 East Fourth Street
Loveland, Colorado 80537 USA
interweavebooks.com

Printed in Canada by Friesens

Library of Congress Cataloging-in-Publication Data
Bush, Nancy, 1951–
    Folk socks : the history & techniques of handknitted footwear / Nancy Bush.
        p.   cm.
    Includes bibliographical references and index.
    ISBN 13: 978-0-934026-97-0
    ISBN 10: 0-934026-97-1
    1. Socks—Europe.   2. Knitting—Patterns.   3. Socks—History.
    I. Title
    TT825.B88   1994
    746.43'20432—dc20   94-5361
                                                                CIP

20 19 18 17 16 15 14 13 12

For Frankie and in Memory of Clary—

parents whose support and love helped make my knitting dreams come true.

ACKNOWLEDGEMENTS

I could fill many pages with thanks to folks who have helped me with this book. Among them are: Brenda Rutledge, Connie Ward, Debra Scott, Vicki Bourg, Joelle Appel, Carol Ellis, Lisa Starobin and Gigi Brandt for allowing me the time away from my retail shop during the last three years to research, write, and knit. Thanks also go to the knitters of Salt Lake City, who have kept me on my toes and given me so much encouragement.

I had invaluable help with translating from Ursula Pimentel, Tone Halverson, John Pearce, Katrin Roop, Rita Tubalkain, and Kerstin Magnuson. Kerstin is also the maker of the wonderful nålbinded socks which illustrate the text. I found inspiration from Latvian knitting lent to me by Raymond Dombrovskis and Lizbeth Upitis, Estonian inspiration enthusiastically shared by Merike Nichols, Norwegian patterns shared by Randi Bjorge, helpful source material lent by Kathe Kliot of Lacis, and from Margaret McLaughlin and my friend Norman Kennedy, whose cassette tapes of traditional Scottish songs and stories kept me entertained during long knitting hours. Thanks to Marsha Thomas for sharing her legal expertise, to Lisa Sewell for proofreading the text while it was under construction, and to Patrick de Freitas for his proofreading, suggestions, comments, international financial transactions, and 'brotherly' encouragement.

I would still be plugging away knitting mates to socks and stockings if I wasn't fortunate enough to have such good friends and expert knitters as Ann Carlile and Michelle Poulin-Alfeld nearby. They proofed the patterns calmly and with care and created matching mates to all my designs.

I had special help from Anu Liivandi at the Royal Ontario Museum in Toronto, Canada; Ellen Värv at the Estonian National Museum in Tartu, Estonia; Jessica Sloane at the Textile Museum in Washington D.C.; Dorothy Lerda at National Geographic in Washington D.C.; Laurann Figg at the Vesterheim Museum in Decorah, Iowa; Lisbeth Green of the Danske Folkedanseres Salgsfdeling; Britta Hammar at the Kulturen Museum in Lund, Sweden; Ingrid Frankow at the Nordiska Museet in Stockholm, Sweden; as well as many curators at various other museums. I offer my gratitude to Linda Burns and her staff at the Interlibrary Loan Department of the Marriott Library at the University of Utah for procuring countless volumes of historic and textile-related books and articles from libraries all over the country.

Many thanks to Robert Brown of The Brown Sheep Company, Deborah Gremlitz of Nordic Fiber Arts, Betsy Marlow and Anne-Marie Fotland of Dale of Norway, and Jim Whitin and Arnold Locher of Renaissance Yarns–Froehlich-wolle for their encouragement, support, and yarns (lots of yarns).

The folks directly responsible for beauty and accuracy of this book work under the roof (either literally or figuratively) of Interweave Press. Grateful thanks to Linda Ligon for seeing that this would work, for her ideas and hospitality; to Judith Durant for her patience and editing abilities. Thanks to Karen Evanson for aid with international transactions, to Barbara Ciletti for teaching me the true meaning of phone tag and for answering my questions with interest and enthusiasm, and to Ann Budd for her keen editorial eye and knitting know-how. Joe Coca's photographs are works of art—they make every sock and stocking glow, and Susan Strawn's illustrations have a life of their own. Debra Cannarella, as editor, did a grand job of making sense of my ramblings, and Dorothy Ratigan, whom I would trust with any precious pattern, made sure that if you follow the instructions written here, you'll end up with the socks pictured in the photographs.

My final thanks, and thanks isn't a broad enough word to really describe how I feel, go to Joe Gardner, my sweetheart, and to Kloo, our furry, barking companion. Without Joe, I would have starved—he kept me fed with gourmet meals (most of the time), told me countless times to "go knit", and shared all the frustration and elation of this project. Our friends are encouraging him to write his own volume—"My Wife was a Sock Addict".

CONTENTS

INTRODUCTION

In 1626, in his play entitled "The Roman Actor", English dramatist Philip Massinger mentions the Greeks "to whome we owe the first invention of the buskined scene and humble sock". Massinger uses these two articles of footwear as symbols to represent the theater (buskins were a type of half-boot and socks, a light shoe worn by ancient Greek and Roman comic actors). For me, however, the key words are "humble sock", for indeed no article of human apparel has been more taken for granted than the sock. And yet, throughout history, language and customs show that they have been an important part of everyday life.

To be "in one's socks" is an indication of stature. To "knock the socks off" means to beat thoroughly. To "pull one's socks up" is to make an effort, and "put a sock in it" is a slightly more polite way than some of the alternatives to ask someone to stop speaking. The term "blue stocking" has become synonymous with literary or intellectual ladies, named for the female members of the mid-eighteenth century Society of Literati, whose founder wore blue stockings (although others say simply that these women were so careless about their dress that they wore the blue, indigo- or woad-dyed stockings common to the working classes). "Old socks" is a familiar way to address someone and "socking away money" is something that has been going on since money was invented (with or without the benefit of a sock to put it in). A lovely example of this use of the sock comes from the 1930 novel *Very Good Jeeves*, by P.G. Wodehouse: "Her name was Maude and he

No article of human apparel has been more taken for granted than the sock ...

loved her dearly, but the family would have none of it. They dug down into the sock and paid her off."

The humble sock also played a central role in those marriages that did take place. Stockings were tossed rather than a floral bouquet. In Britain, to "throw the stocking" had special meaning for wedding guests. On the wedding night, the bride's stocking was thrown among the guests, and the "lucky" person struck by it would be the next to be married. (The garter has taken the place of the sock in modern ritual—probably because it's easier to get off.) In another version, the bride and groom would retire to bed, fully dressed but for their stockings and shoes. Their friends would appear and, with their backs to the blissful couple, take turns in trying to hit either the groom or the bride with one of their own stockings. The first bridesmaid and groomsman to succeed would, in theory, celebrate their own weddings before the year was out. In Scotland, when a younger sister contracted to marry, she would send her elder, unmarried sister a pair of green stockings for her to wear to the dance—green means forsaken. The Scottish elder sister had it better than one in Shropshire and other parts of England, however, as the latter had to go to the dance barefooted!

I have spent years researching knitting traditions and ethnic patterns, learning how knitters of old created their masterpieces. I had never given the sock a thought, until one day, while observing a man in a kilt, complete with all the accessories necessary to a well-dressed Scot, I realized that his stockings were knitted. I thought, "Wouldn't it be lovely if they were hand knitted?" But they weren't. So began my research into the mysteries of kilt hose. This experience led me to wonder further about socks and stockings in general, and this book is a compilation of what I have discovered.

Knitting for me is more than a hobby or a livelihood. It is a means of binding my life together with the lives of all the knitters, men and women, who have knit before me—from those individuals who discovered how to make interlocking loops with fingers and hooked ends of sticks, to those country folk who made their livelihood selling hand-knit stockings far from their own land. The traditions inspire me, as do the stories, the bits of

Woman and Child from Kihnu, 1951
The true character of the humble sock comes from the knitters who knit
as they walked down country lanes or across fields . . .

climate, but also the making of them, because wool has always been in great supply. I have written the technical chapters with the beginning sock knitter in mind and have included additional information that I hope anyone who is interested in knitting socks and stockings will enjoy and benefit from.

The patterns are selected from historical, ethnic socks and stockings. I agree with Sir Walter Scott who said that "the character of a nation is not to be learnt from its fine folks". The true character of the humble sock comes from the knitters who worked by the light of a peat fire, who knit as they walked down country lanes or across fields,

folklore, and the varied patterns that have been created out of a need for warmth, for fashion, to tell a story, or simply for pleasure.

In searching out sock lore and fact, I have focused my research mostly on Northern Europe, a place very conducive not only to the wearing of stockings, because of the

who dreamed up lovely colored patterns and decorated their simple finery with knitted stitches that twisted, turned, took on the pattern of stars, crowns, birds, and flowers. I have always been a lover of folk art, and I consider the socks and stockings that I have included here as inspiration for true folk art—the art of the people.

FROM HIDE TO HOSE

The origins of the sock

—⟐—

The history of the humble sock is a long and interesting one. No one knows exactly when man first found he would be more comfortable if his feet were covered. Perhaps as he sat huddled beneath an animal skin and tucked a part of it over his feet, it occurred to him to wrap and bind small skins around each foot for better protection from the cold and coarse ground.

The concept of a sock does not appear in the writings of any people in any language prior to the eighth century B.C. Milton Grass' *History of Hosiery* tells us that in the hieroglyphics of Ancient Egypt, the cuneiform writings of Babylonians and Assyrians, or in the Old Testament of the Hebrew Bible, there is no word that describes an inner foot covering or what we have come to recognize as a sock or stocking today.

One of the earliest written mentions of a socklike article occurs in a poem entitled "Works and Days", attributed to the Greek poet Hesiod, who lived about 700 B.C. Hesiod describes the joys and troubles of the farmer's everyday life and warns of cold weather, advising the farmer, "And on your feet bind boots of the hide of the slaughtered ox, fitting them closely, when you have cushioned their insides with felt". "Felt" is the translation of the Greek word *pilos* (*piloi*, pl.), which later referred to any article made from felt. The origin is an older word meaning "hair". The technique of matting animal hair into felt was very likely known to man before spinning or weaving, so this reference is probably to a felted, perhaps shaped, piece made from animal hair, worn on or over the foot, inside a shoe or sandal.

Although there are no written references until shortly before the start of the first century A.D., it is very likely that some form of sock was worn by the people of the

> **"***And on your feet bind boots of the hide of the slaughtered ox, fitting them closely, when you have cushioned their insides with felt***"**
>
> HESIOD

Roman Empire, due to trade and exchange with the Greeks. The Latin word *fascia* (*fasciae*, pl.) is defined as "a strip of material, bandage, ribbon band or puttee worn around the legs and ankles". *Fasciae* were made of cloth or leather and covered the shin and leg (these were *fascia crurales*) and sometimes the foot. They were commonly worn by older men and women as protection from the cold, but considered a sign of weakness when worn by men who were not on military duty.

Vindolanda cloth sock

According to Grass, by the first century A.D. attitudes had changed and fascia were worn by men as a sign of affluence. This change of attitude is mentioned by Horatius (65 to 8 B.C.) in his *Satires*, where he notes that leg bindings were common attire for men at this time. Valerius Maximus, in his first-century history of manners, stated that white fasciae, worn by men, were a sign of extraordinary refinement in dress. Around 50 B.C., when the Romans headed north to Gaul, they discovered that the barbaric Gauls, as well as the Britons, were wrapping cloth or leather strips around their bare legs or loose breeches (*braccae* [Latin] or *broc* [Anglo Saxon]) to protect themselves from cold and from the thickets of the forest. The Romans adapted these leg coverings, called them *tibialae*, and brought the fashion home.

During the first century A.D., it became more acceptable for men to wear leg coverings, and the concept of a total foot and leg covering began to emerge. According to Grass, *Udo* (*udones*, pl.) is "a kind of felt slipper or sock of felt or fur". An *udo* differs from a *fascia* or *tibiale* as it was pulled on rather than wrapped around the foot and leg, and was cut from fabric or skin rather than made from strips of cloth or leather.

A discovery made at Vindolanda in Northumberland, England, sheds new light on the ancient practice of wearing socks. In 1973, the first of hundreds of inked tablets, dating from the first century A.D., were found there. Vindolanda, a Roman site near Hadrian's Wall, was home to officers, soldiers, and their families, who were sent to guard Roman holdings in North Britain. These tablets, made of thin leaves of wood, served as letters and documents sent from officials and family members to the residents of Vindolanda. One tablet, regrettably only a fragment of the original, appears to be a letter to a soldier, although it's not known who sent it or to whom it was addressed: "I have sent you . . . pairs of socks (*udonum*) from Sattua, two pairs of sandals and two sets of underpants" and continues on with greetings to fellow soldiers. This is the first written evidence that socks were worn in this northern climate.

A socklike article of clothing was also found at Vindolanda. Believed to have belonged to a child, it is described in letters from J.P. Wild, professor of Archaeology at Manchester University, Manchester, England, as similar to a "small bootee, reaching up to the ankle bone and constructed of two pieces of diamond twill cloth in wool, one acting as the 'upper', the other as the 'sole'. There are signs of a good deal of wear on the heel, and it was presumably worn inside a sandal." Dr. Wild also indicated that cloth socks were common during the Roman period.

Grass tells us that the word *udo* appeared again in the second century A.D. in what sounds like an advertisement: "Wool did not supply these [*udone*] but the beard of the he-goat. Your feet will be able to take refuge, in cloth made of goat's hair, which came from Cinyps." Cinyps was a river in Africa, and reportedly the best quality of goat's hair came from this region.

After the fall of Rome in the mid-fifth century, the Saxons gained control of Britain. The Saxons wore a type of loose tunic and either long or short (to the knee) tight-fitting pants or *broc*. The Saxon continued to bind his bare legs with leg guards, or the longer drawers with woven cloth or leather, called *scanc-beorg*. They also wore a short sock made of cloth or thin leather called a *stocc* or *socque* (Anglo Saxon) or *soccus* (Latin). This costume was common in Europe from the fifth to the eleventh centuries.

By the sixth century, loose breeches, *bracco, broc,* or *braies* (French) were generally adopted. They were made of linen, wool, or hide and were frequently cross gartered, that is, wrapped with cloth or leather. These trouserlike garments became tighter fitting over time, with the lower part (from the knee down) fitting closer to the leg. By the beginning of the twelfth century, these breeches were eventually shortened to the knee, and the lower leg was covered with its own separate garment, *chausses* (French) or *hose* (Anglo Saxon). These coarsely cut and sewn hose, made of linen or wool, were fitted to the leg and seamed up the back. They were either footed or footless or had a stirrup under the foot. Those with feet sometimes had leather or felt soles attached. Shoemaking was a highly skilled craft by the 12th century, and therefore shoes were also worn on bare or stockinged feet. Men's hose were knee length and sometimes had an embroidered border at the knee. Women's hose were similar, but reached above the knee and fastened with ties. These hose eventually replaced leg bindings, even though the use of leg bindings continued among some inhabitants of Europe for hundreds of years and, as in parts of Scandinavia, even into this century.

By the early fourteenth century in Europe, hose were worn in various lengths: just below the calf, to the knee, or to the thigh. They were more decorative than in previous times, with the legs often striped in different colors or each a different color. Soled hose continued to be worn until the late fifteenth century. Exaggerated toes became the fashion of the late fourteenth century. They were called "long pikes" or "cracowes". The toes were stuffed with wool, tow linen, or even moss. The shoes, boots, or soled hose were sometimes decorated at the instep with lacings or jeweled patterns. These decorations were the forerunners of "clocks", which decorated knitted stockings of later times.

The slight freedom or stretch of the hose was created by cutting the plain-weave fabric on the bias—the warp and weft would then lie on a diagonal across the vertical. Advances in textile manufacture was one of the factors allowing for this change in fashion. Among the more flexible materials produced, scarlet was a fine elastic wool fabric, very suitable for making hose. It was dyed in many colors, red being the most successful and most common. This red has come to be known as the color scarlet today.

These garments, *chausses* (French), *heuse* (German) or *hose* (Anglo-Norman—by this time, 1066, the Normans had conquered Britain), played an important role in the evolution of costume, particularly for men. Women wore long gowns, and their leg coverings were hidden from view by yards of flowing fabric. Fashion, however, shortened men's tunics to jackets, which grew shorter still. As this occurred, men's hose took on a new role. Breeches were abandoned altogether and the hose took their place, extending up the legs to meet at the crotch. These "tights" were attached to the jacket by points, short laces with tagged metal ends, which were tied through holes pierced at the tops of the hose. Variations on this system of attaching or trussing hose to the jacket or doublet continued into the 1600s.

People have often wondered about the fashion of their own time, and they surely did so now. By the beginning

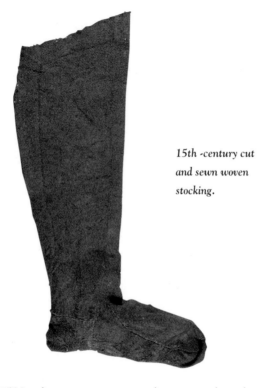

15th-century cut and sewn woven stocking.

both stockings met. The codpiece was stuffed with canvas or hair and had a lining of silk or other fabric. It was often used as a purse or pocket.

The next refinement was the division of stockings and breeches. Although still attached to each other, the upper part or upperstocks were appliquéd, slashed, and puffed, and the lower part, the netherstocks or stockings of hose, were sometimes gartered with ribbons at the knee.

The upperstocks became the focal point of the costume. They were made from patterned fabrics or decorated with embroidery or braid. Eventually they were cut with vertical slits to allow a lining of contrasting color or underhose to be seen beneath the outer fabric. Upperstocks evolved into trunk hose around the mid 1500s, which were also known as slops, round hose, or French hose. At first, trunk hose were onion shaped, beginning at the waistline and extending to the middle of the thigh. Canions, which were tight, tubal extensions resembling biking shorts, were worn with them. The stockings were pulled over the canions above the knee or tucked under them and tied with ribbons or gartered. As time passed, trunk hose became even more elaborate—patterned, stitched, and slit to an extreme. These trunk hose were often puffed out and stuffed with straw or horsehair to give incredible bulk. The codpiece was part of this costume until the late 1500s when it lost fashion's favor.

By the late sixteenth century, true breeches, called venetians, were becoming common. A Spanish fashion popularized by the Venetians and eventually adopted by the rest of Europe, these breeches took many forms—from baggy or skin-tight to inverted pear-shaped shorts. Venetians ended just below the knee and were worn with stockings held up by garters. These stockings, similar to those familiar to us today, were different from cut-and-seamed fabric hose as the fabric was made using a remarkable technique, known as knitting.

of the 1500s, the two separate articles worn as hose had become one garment reaching from waist to ankle and sometimes covering the feet. These hose were often made of fine silk, wool, or velvet, brightly colored, and decorated with embroidery and patterning. Often each leg had a different pattern or color or the tops of the hose were patterned to look like a separate garment. They showed every muscle and every flaw the wearer possessed. Even writers of the day labeled the style immodest.

To add to an already overwhelming display in men's fashion, the jacket became shorter still and the codpiece was added. This refinement was a movable flap or "bag" attached to the front of men's hose by points or buckles to cover as well as to attract attention to the place where

LOOPED FABRICS AND THE LEGWEAR OF QUEENS

The beginnings of knitting and knitted hose

Knitting is the interlacing of a single thread into a series of connected loops to create a fabric. It is not known where or when the art of hand-knitting was first practiced, but the oldest surviving examples of what has been identified as knitted textile fragments date from before A.D. 256. They were discovered at the site of the ancient Syrian fortress city of Dura Europos, which was founded around 280 B.C. by soldiers of Alexander the Great. Because of its location on the Euphrates River, the city became a crossroads for caravans and an important trading center. Although conquered by the Parthians and later by the Romans, in A.D. 256, the Persians finally destroyed the city. The items they left behind were covered by the desert sands.

Three wool fragments found there, now in the collection of Yale University in New Haven, Connecticut, are made of what appears to be knitted stitches. There is no information as to what types of articles these fragments were part of or where they originated. In fact, the fabrics could have been made elsewhere and transported to Dura to be sold or traded in the markets. Many scholars, judging from the dating of coins also found on the site of Dura Europos, claim that they are the oldest existing examples of knitting. In "The Excavations at Dura-Europos, Final Report IV, Part II, The Textiles", authors Pfister and Bellinger describe these three fragments as true knitting worked in Crossed Eastern Stitch, or crossed knitting.

In crossed knitting, the stitches are made by knitting into the back of the stitch rather than the front. The stitch is then twisted, which forms a cross. The left side of the stitch

The oldest surviving examples of what has been identified as knitted textile fragments date from before A.D. 256. They were discovered at the site of the ancient Syrian fortress city of Dura Europos.

may cross over to the right or the right side to the left, but the direction of the crossing is identical on the two sides of the fabric (Irene Emery, *The Primary Structure of Fabrics*).

In her article on Coptic (Egyptian) knitting, published in 1972, Dorothy Burnham discusses a comparable technique used to create a number of socks found in Egypt and dating from the fourth and fifth centuries A.D. Although these socks were also originally believed to be crossed-knit, Burnham asserts they were made by single-needle looping. "The appearance of the socks is similar to ordinary knitting, but with a twist in each stitch. This might be explained by the use of the so-called Crossed Eastern Knitting, but the start and finish of the socks and many other constructional peculiarities could not have been produced this way."

To support her theory, Burnham explains that no object similar to knitting needles had been found among the household artifacts with the socks, yet many needles of bronze and bone similar to darning needles were found nearby. Through experimentation, she discovered that by using a darning needle and short, separate lengths of yarn, she could reproduce exactly the construction of the Coptic socks. The resulting fabric looks like that made with the Crossed Eastern Stitch, but does not unravel in the same manner as true knitting.

Although these Coptic textiles may not have been knitted, they are looped wool fabrics, constructed in the shape of foot coverings and recognizable as socks. Each has a shaped heel, a tube-shaped leg, and a separation between the big toe and the rest of the foot to allow the wearing of a thong type of sandal.

The process of single-needle looping is a slow one. The short lengths of yarn need to be joined in at frequent intervals, which forces the maker to interrupt the rhythm of the work. Pulling out to correct a mistake is a slow and frustrating experience. In comparison to single-needle looping, knitting can be worked quickly, joining in short ends of yarn is not necessary, and the resulting fabric is perfectly suited to garments that need to fit snugly yet stretch to be put on, such as socks, gloves, and caps. Once these advantages were evident, knitting no doubt grew in popularity and the knitters in skill.

Fragments from Dura Europos

As cited in Irene Turnau's *History of Knitting Before Mass Production*, J.P. Wild described a knitted fragment found in what is now Holland, and two ivory needles, similar to knitting needles, found near Nimes, France, all dating from the end of the second century A.D. However, if, indeed, knitting hadn't been invented by the fourth or fifth century, it was surely discovered soon after.

The oldest fragments that are positively true knitting as we know it have been dated no earlier than A.D. 600 to A.D. 800. These early knitted pieces were liturgical gloves, which were worn by bishops and made from wool or silk and, rarely, linen. A silk textile, depicted in *Mary Thomas's Knitting Book*, which had belonged to the Swiss collector Fritz Ikle but has been lost, was found at Fustat (modern Cairo). The stranded pattern knitting is described as being worked in Crossed Eastern Stitch at 36 stitches per inch, and is a fine example of skilled craftsmanship. Though the piece was originally thought to date from the seventh to the ninth centuries, it may have been created later. Similar examples of Islamic knitting date to the twelfth century or later.

Many Islamic stockings and other knitted fragments date from the thirteenth to sixteenth centuries. Like the Coptic socks mentioned earlier, many were worked from the toe upward, hand-knit with needles that may or may not have had hooked points, in colored patterns that often incorporated the name "Allah" in Kufic (an early Arabic script) or the Roman letter N, the significance of which is unknown to me, and its mirror image.

From this scant evidence, one can conclude that *true* knitting began somewhere between A.D. 500 and A.D. 1200, in Egypt or another Arabic country. For the most part, this early knitting was for socks or stockings, and was done mostly in the round. The maker added decoration with stranded-color knitting.

KNITTING IN EUROPE

As people traveled, traded, and conquered new lands, so too did skills and ideas migrate from place to place. Missionaries and monks were traveling and carrying with them more than just their beliefs. Many Europeans were discovering new ideas and skills as a result of the Crusades— circa 1095–1291. Knitting also might have found its way into Europe with sailors or soldiers. It is also possible that the craft was carried into Europe through Muslim expansion into Spain which began around A.D. 710.

As the craft of knitting began to spread throughout Europe, the logic of making knitted hose rather than woven, cut, and sewn hose certainly became evident. Although the old style of woven hose were still worn, knitted stockings became increasingly popular. Knitted fabric was superior to woven cloth because it retained its shape and fit better and it offered new options in design and color.

Turnau cites written sources from France in 1387 that mention three pairs of *chausses* (stockings) of fine *escarlete faictes a l'esguille* (scarlet made with needles). These

Arab Stocking

In royal costume, every detail of dress was important, and stockings were not ignored. They were dyed to match doublets and other accessories and were often embroidered with ornate designs in silk or other precious threads.

early stockings were wool or linen, coarsely made with large needles.

As skill in metalwork advanced, primarily in Spain and Italy, finer needles allowed for finer knit work. Two cushions from the late thirteenth century, knit in a fine-gauge Stockinette stitch and decorated with stranded-pattern motifs, were discovered in royal tombs in Burgos in Northern Spain. In his book, *History of Hand Knitting,* Richard Rutt describes these cushions in detail. He believes they are the product of the combination of Muslim heritage and Hispano-Arab skill in steel work, which produced the fine-gauge needles necessary for such skilled craftsmanship.

The Spanish and the Italians became very skilled at fine-gauge knitting. William Harrison in his *Description of England (1577-1587)* makes reference to Spanish stockings. "The Spanish now wear trunk hose . . . and beneath them curiously wrought stockings." These "curiously wrought", i.e. knitted, stockings were quite probably made of silk.

SILK STOCKINGS OF THE ARISTOCRACY

A pair of these special Spanish stockings were prized possessions of Henry VIII of England who reigned from 1509-1547. Apparently Henry wore cut, sewn, and seamed cloth hose, made of woven fabric, probably wool or "taffety", the glossy silk we now call taffeta. In John Stow's *annals or general chronicles of England* edited by Howes (1615), it is noted that "by great chance, there came a payre of

Spanish silke stockings from Spain" into Henry's possession. These stockings must have been special to be mentioned as clothing for a king who was already known for his sumptuous dress.

In royal costume, every detail of dress was important, and stockings were not ignored. They were dyed to match doublets and other accessories and were often embroidered with ornate designs in silk or other precious threads. According to Howes, Henry's successor Edward VI, who reigned from 1547–1553, had a "payre of long Spanish silke stockings sent him for a great present". They were a gift from Sir Thomas Gresham, an importer of Spanish stockings into England, who continued his business during the reign of Elizabeth I. Knitted stockings were also worn by Mary Stuart (Queen of Scots reigning from 1542–1567). When she was executed in 1586, she was wearing two pair of knitted stockings. One was a "pair of Jersey hose white worn under nether stocks of worsted, coloured watchett, clocked with silver". The white Jersey hose were held up with green garters. Mary I (reigning 1553-1558) probably had access to knitted Spanish stockings through her marriage to Philip II of Spain in 1554. In that year, she received 27 pairs of cloth hose from her hosier Myles Huggarde. Two years later she was given gifts of four pairs of hose "of Garnsey making" by Sir Leonard Chamberlain, the governor of Guernsey.

The wealthy also discovered the luxury of knitted stockings. Eleanora of Toledo, wife of the Grand Duke of Tuscany Cosimo I de'Medici, was buried in 1562 wearing a pair of ornate crimson silk stockings. Turnau tells of three

Coronation stockings of Gustavus II Adolphus, 1617.

silk stockings found in the coffins of the Pomeranian princes beneath the castle at Szczecin, Poland in 1946. Two of these form a pair. They are of dark brown silk (which was probably originally black), worked carefully in Stockinette stitch, but otherwise plain. They are quite long and would reach above the wearer's knees. These stockings are believed to have been made around 1600, possibly at the court of Prince Barnim XII in whose coffin they were found, or in England or Spain as these societies were excelling in stocking-knitting by this time. The third stocking is larger and has small holes at the top for the tapes that attach the stocking above the knee. This stocking, probably from the late 1500s, shows Spanish influence which is typical for the costumes worn by the princes at this time. The fashion for men stressed a well-shaped leg, which lent itself well to the tight fit and elastic qualities of knitted fabric. The Spanish influence in courtly manners and proper court dress was evident throughout Europe. Knitted silk stockings even found their way north into Sweden. An inventory from the wardrobe of King Erik XIV (born 1533, died 1577) reveals that in 1566 the king owned at least 27 pairs of stockings, mostly made of silk. These items of courtly dress varied in color: red, violet, yellow, pink, brown, black, and gray. One of King Erik's pair of silk stockings, imported in 1562, cost the same as the annual wages for a chamber valet, as noted by Susanne Pagoldh in *Nordic Knitting*. King Erik's son Johan III, who became king in

1569, also had a large collection of stockings. According to Gudrun Ekstrand in an article entitled "Some Early Silk Textiles in Sweden", when his tomb was opened in 1945-1946, the pair of silk stockings in which he had been buried in 1594 were discovered, yellow with age. They are nearly 22 inches long, worked in stockinette stitch with a purl stitch "seam" at the back. An exceptionally beautiful pair of silk stockings were worn by Gustavus II Adolphus, who lived from 1594 to 1632, during his coronation in 1617. They are hand knit of white silk and measure approximately 26" long. There are 25 stitches 32 rows to an inch, indicating craftsmanship of amazing skill. The tops are turned down and are lined with white taffeta and have holes for attaching the stockings to breeches with ribbons. The back seam is embroidered with silver and there is ornate embroidery of silver thread and cords at the ankles.

By the time Elizabeth I took the throne in England in 1558, knitting was becoming a widespread craft. Howes mentions the Queen's receipt of her first pair of silk stockings in his revision of Stow's *annals*, a romantic, if not altogether accurate depiction, as he wrote it over 50 years after it was said to occur. He notes that in 1560, Elizabeth's silk woman, Mistress Montague (or Montagu), gave the Queen a pair of black knit silk stockings for a New Year's gift. Elizabeth liked them so well that she asked Mistress Montague if she could acquire any more. Montague replied,

Italian children's stockings. Knitted silk with embroidery.

"I made them very carefully of purpose only for Your Majesty; and seeing these please you so well, I will presently get more in hand." Montague had her work cut out for her as the Queen is quoted as saying, "Do so, for indeed I like silk stockings so well, because they are so pleasant, fine and delicate, that henceforth I will wear no more cloth stockings."

Elizabeth's early silk stockings were black, but by 1588 she was wearing stockings of carnation pink and other colors, "wrought at the clockes with venice gold and silver"(Jeremy Farrell, *Socks and Stockings*). She also wore woven linen understockings beneath her silk hose, to protect them from wear and perspiration.

Howes notes that, true to her declaration, from the time of her gift from Mistress Montague to the time of her death, the Queen only wore silk stockings. However, Farrell reports that the Queen was supplied with about 20 pairs of cloth hose a year until 1577, at which time she switched to knitted wool hose made in Norwich, an area known for worsted weaving and knitting.

THREE

KNITTING IN GREAT BRITAIN

A way of working and a way of life

✣

By the early sixteenth century, knitted wool stockings were worn mostly by England's children and country people, but by the middle of the century, the time of Elizabeth I, they were worn by the aristocracy as well. As the masses followed the styles and acquired the tastes of the well-dressed, wool stockings became increasingly popular.

The fashion in the 1500s for men's dress was knee-length breeches which created a need for stockings of all types—woolen, silk, linen, and cotton, plain or patterned, rough or fine. Women also wore stockings, and while they were often not seen under full-length skirts, they were a necessary part of daily life. Technical terms for leg wear were changing, too. After about 1550, hose referred to breeches and legs were covered with hand-knit netherstocks or stockings. By the mid 1600s, the terms hose and stockings were synonymous.

Howes offers his version of the introduction of knitted worsted wool stockings in England: "In the year 1564 William Rider, being an apprentice with Master Thomas Burdett at the bridge foot over against St. Magnus Church, chanced to see a pair of knit worsted stockings in the lodging of an Italian merchant that came from Mantua. He borrowed these stockings and caused other stockings to be made by them; and these were the first worsted stockings made in England. . . . Within a few years began the plenteous making both of jersey and woolen stockings, so in a short space they waxed common" (Rutt, *The History of Hand Knitting*).

The fashion in the 1500s for men's dress was knee-length breeches which created a need for stockings of all types—woolen, silk, linen, and cotton, plain and patterned, rough or fine.

Throughout all of Britain, stockings were being knit. Each area produced a different type of stocking, depending on the type of wool available. Stockings made in Yorkshire were coarse and hard wearing and were worn by farm workers, soldiers, and children. Welsh and Cornish stockings were similar. Finer worsted stockings from the Midlands were worn by merchants and townspeople.

In addition to being made with many types and grades

The knitting of stockings

gave many peasant

laborers an independence

they could not have had

otherwise.

Girl knitting on West Pier, Whitby

of wool, stockings were available in many styles and colors and in short or long lengths, reaching to the knees or extending above them. They were sometimes plain or sometimes fancy, with decorative scalloped ribbing or welts, or embroidered at the ankle with decorative designs called clocks. The name for these designs has obscure origins, but is believed to come from the design's resemblance to the hands or pendulum of a clock.

Philip Stubbs in his *Anatome of Abuses* (1595) described the fashion of the day; "Then they have nether stockes to these gay hosen, not of cloth (though never so fine) for that is thought too base, but of jarnsey, worsted, crewell, silke, thread and such like, or else, at the least, of the finest yarn that can be got; and so curiously knit with open seame down the leg, with quirkes and clocks about the ankles, and sometime (haplie) interlaced about the ancles with gold or silver thread as is wonderful to behold." He goes on to report on the excesses that people were willing to exhibit when it came to purchasing and wearing stockings; "And to such impudent insolency and shameful outrage it is now growne, that everyone almost, though otherwise very poor, having scarce forty shillings wages by the year, will not stick to have two or three pair of these silk nether stocks, or else of the finest yarn that may be got, though price of them be royal, or twenty shillings, or more, as commonly it is; for how can they be lesse, when as the very knitting of them is worth a noble or a royal, and some much more? The time hath been when one might have clothed all his body well, from top to toe, for lesse than a pair of these nether stocks will cost."

THE DEVELOPMENT OF AN INDUSTRY

Due to their popularity and usefulness, the knitting of stockings, socks, caps, and other articles of clothing offered a source of livelihood for many people, thereby becoming an industry in its own right.

The knitting of stockings gave many peasant laborers an independence they could not have had otherwise. Most mastered their skill and worked for themselves. They lived in rural communities, farmed the land, and had enough time to supplement their income with this extra employment.

A knitting school opened in York in 1588 and another in Lincoln in 1591, which thrived through the seventeenth century. Other schools were started, in both rural and town sites, with the objective of helping the poor and providing a skill for idle hands prone to mischief.

An anonymous writer in 1615 described the old and new ways of spinning and weaving wool. In the old way, spinners and weavers worked for a clothier and made very small wages. In the new way, wool was of a finer quality and lighter weight, made by better paid and more highly skilled workers. Stockings were made in the new way. A new clip of wool was divided into thirds: two thirds to be used for woven woolen goods, one third for stockings. According to Joan Thirsk in her article, "The Fantastical Folly of Fashion", three times the number of people were required to make wool in the new way than were required before, and their wages were four times as much as before. The spinning wheel had taken the place of the spindle and distaff in the late 1500s, and yarn was then produced in sufficient quantities to keep the busy knitters supplied.

Thirsk estimates that, in the sixteenth century, the population of the United Kingdom was between 4.5 and 5.5 million. She reasonably assumes that everyone wore out at least two pairs of stockings a year. By this estimate, somewhere between 9 and 11 million pairs of stockings had to be produced every year. Many people did not make their own stockings. In 1595, the collectors of aulnage (excise duty for woolen cloth) reasoned that one knitter made two pairs of stockings per week. Taking all this into ac-

Knitting sheaths

count, the domestic market alone would have provided work for fifty weeks a year for around 90,000 to 110,000 people.

Stockings were not only made to be worn at home in Britain. By the end of the 1600s, one to two million pairs of stockings were being exported from Britain into other parts of Europe. Most of these stockings were knitted, though some were made of kersey (a coarse cloth woven in a twill pattern, resistant to wet and cold).

THE KNITTING MACHINE

The first knitting machine was invented by William Lee in 1589. There is much speculation as to how he was inspired to create his stocking frame. There were surely knitters living near his home in Calverton in Nottinghamshire, and romantic stories tell of how he watched his sweetheart knitting stockings and, feeling ignored by her,

invented the frame to make her work go more quickly, thereby allowing her to spend more of her time with him.

Lee presented his frame for wool stockings to Queen Elizabeth, who, at that time, was more interested in silk stockings. By 1599 Lee perfected the making of silk stockings on his frame, and although he had some success in England, he decided he could do better in France. Promised an introduction to the king, who he was sure would help him, Lee settled in Rouen. But after the king was assassinated and Lee's hopes of royal patronage dissolved, he died a disappointed man. Before his death, however, Lee had taught a number of workers to use his invention, including his brother James, who had gone to France with him.

After William's death, James went back to Nottingham and began making machine-knit worsted stockings. Frame knitters eventually began to live in towns. They farmed less, worked for a lower wage, and did not have the independence they had as hand knitters. This simple mechanization was the first of many changes in the textile industry, which continued to unfold up to and throughout the Industrial Revolution almost three hundred years later.

By the mid 1600s, the needs of the knitting industry were met by three categories of workers; silk-frame knitters, who were centered in London; wool-frame knitters in the Midlands; and the remaining hand knitters dispersed throughout the rural areas of Yorkshire, Wales, Scotland, the Channel Islands, and other areas.

THE HAND KNITTERS
OF THE YORKSHIRE DALES

By 1900, in the remote villages and farms of Dentdale and Wensleydale, in the Yorkshire Dales of England, hand knitting had been a daily employment for three centuries. Practiced by women, children, and men, the craft added much to the economy of the Dales people. Most of the items knitted were stockings, but caps, mittens, and gloves were also produced. Richmond and Kendal were the centers of trade, from which goods were shipped to other parts of Britain, the Netherlands, the West Indies, and the American Colonies.

These knitters worked at great speed, using a knitting sheath to support one of the needles, called wires or pricks, and rocking back and forth while knitting to give the work a rhythm. While they knit, the fabric was supported by hooks of different shapes. One end of the hook was attached to the knitter's apron, the other to the knitting. A clue-holder was used to support a ball or clue of wool, or the ball was pinned to the apron with a safety pin, or attached to the knitter by suspending it with a length of yarn. The yarn was either wound into a ball on a wooden stick similar to a Norwegian nøstepinne or wound around a thropple. This curious tool was made from the windpipe of a goose into which dried peas or small stones were placed. It was then formed into a circle like the letter O and became a sort of rattle. If this "clue" was lost in the dark, the knitter could easily find it by its rattling. Variations of these tools were used throughout Britain and other countries.

William Howitt, who lived in nineteenth-century Victorian England, chronicled his time with sentiment and keen observation in *The Rural Life of England*. In the Dales he discovered some curious knitting practices: "They sit rocking to and fro like so many weird wizards. They burn no candle, but knit by the light of the peat fire. And this rocking motion is connected with a mode of knitting peculiar to the place, called swav-

ing, which is difficult to describe. Ordinary knitting is performed by a variety of little motions, but this is a single uniform tossing motion of both the hands at once, the body often accompanying it with a sort of sympathetic action . . . . They knit with crooked pins called pricks; and use a knitting-sheath of a dagger, curved to the side, and fixed in a belt called the cowband" (Souden, *Victorian Village*).

In his "Memorial by the Trustees of Cowgill Chapel", Adam Sedgewick describes the life he knew in the Dales. Although he lived during a time when modern ways were affecting the traditions of the past, he had memories from his youth of a life filled with those traditions. "Wool must have been a great staple of the valley from its earliest history. The greater part was exported; but some was retained for domestic use; (which in my childhood, I have seen in actual use); and then spun into a very coarse and clumsy thread; and so it supplied the material for a kind of rude

Yarn or Clue Holder

manufacture that went, I think, under the elegant name of *bump*." Sedgewick remembers the habits and manners of the women, and noted that their industry had a "social character", that they were "lively gossips" and "worked together in little clusters—not in the din and confinement of a modern manufactory". He described a sitting, or gathering of neighbors around a fire in wintertime, which may be the source of all the romantic notions of how one should spend one's knitting time. He describes the room and the furniture, the "blazing fire composed of turf and great logs of wood". He notes that the surroundings were "rude," but "in it no sign of want" and had many "signs of rural comfort".

"They took their seats; and then began the work of the evening; and with a speed that cheated the eye, they went on with their respective tasks. Beautiful gloves were thrown off complete; and worsted stockings made good progress. There was no dreary deafening noise of machinery; but there was the merry heart-cheering sound of the human tongue. No one could foretell the current of the evenings talk. They had their ghost tales; and their ancient songs of enormous length, yet heard by ears that were never weary. Each in turn was to play its part, according to the humor of the Sitting."

HAND KNITTERS OF WALES

Knitting also had social significance in the rural Welsh knitter's life, well described in Hugh Evan's *Cum Eithin*. The knitting night (*noson weu* or *noswaith weu*) was an important social event in eighteenth-century Wales and well into the nineteenth century. The party was often held on moonlit nights with special treats provided by the hostess. The ladies usually arrived first and the young men followed later. All the ladies would work on their knitting; some of the men would knit garters. Both written and oral accounts show that not much work was really accomplished during these evenings—stories were told and stitches were dropped as teasing lads pulled out needles. Good storytellers were always welcome at these gatherings, especially if they told ghost stories, which made the ladies nervous and unwilling to walk home without a male escort (from Minwel Tibbott's *Knitting Stockings in Wales*).

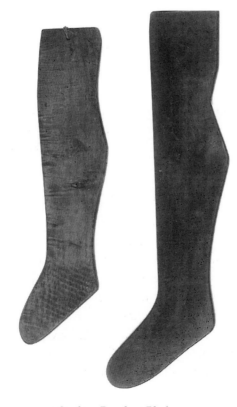

Stocking Boards or Blockers

Knitting had as important a place in the rural economy of Wales as it did elsewhere in Britain. People were poor and had to work hard and live frugally to survive. Trevor Owen in *Customs and Traditions of Wales* notes that thrift was essential and mentions the Welsh belief that

Waist Hooks

"there were three ways which led to the workhouse, namely buying peat, buying bread and buying fresh meat". Work was found wherever possible, and cooperation and charity between neighbors was important. Owen tells about a man on Anglesey who was employed as a thresher during the winter, and whose payment of corn fed him and his pig throughout the year. He spent his winter evenings peeling and combing the hemp from his garden, preparing it for his wife to spin, and making clogs and baskets. His wife also spun wool, for which she traded the medicines she made from herbs grown in her garden. The garden also supplied vegetables, which was the staple of their diet. They raised chickens and a pig, and kept a corgi and a cat as pets. The wife also knitted stockings—a common way of supplementing income. Even the children earned some wages knitting.

The period around the autumnal equinox marked the beginning of *cadw dechreunos* or "keeping the evening". The first candle of the autumn was lit, and the family gathered around the hearth. Now, after the labors of summer were done, there was time to work on domestic crafts. Woolen hose, knitted by people of all ages, was a staple commodity. Owen states that, "This is a source of useful employment, and a happy mode of procuring a livelihood for the poor whom it is common to meet on the roads, travelling upon other business, busily at work with their knitting needles. . . ."

Wool gathering, or *gwlana*, was another social custom adopted to provide for poorer women or the wives of laborers who did not have access to wool of their own to spin and then knit or weave into clothing. Generally, gwlana took place at the end of the shearing season. The women would travel along set routes, called *llwybrau gwlân* or woolen paths, visiting farmers' wives who had set some sheared fleece aside to give to the gatherers. The gatherers would carry the wool in pillowcases on their backs.

Wool gathering was also done by walking along the hedgerows and stone walls and picking off the wool that was left as the sheep passed by. Usually the women would form a small party of six or so and carry supplies with them for a week or more. They would go from the urban lowlands to the hills and request permission to search for wool on the farmer's lands.

These women would gather from two to four pounds of wool in a day, travelling from as early as four o'clock in the morning. They would find more wool if there had been a severe winter followed by a good spring. Friendships formed between the remote farm families and the women of the towns, and often the wool gatherers would help with the farm chores at the end of the day in exchange for food and shelter.

By the nineteenth century, the gathered wool might have been spun at a local mill, rather than by hand. It would then be woven or knitted at home into clothing for the family or to sell at market. The wool for stockings was usually dyed before it was spun, sometimes after, and sometimes even after the stockings had been knit. Men wore a blue-gray color called pot-blue and women and children wore black-dyed stockings. A speckled yarn could be created by binding skeins of undyed yarn with rush-peel, a plant fiber, and soaking them in a mixture of lichen, water, and sour urine that had been boiled.

According to Tibbott, stockings made for the family were knit in a ribbed pattern, "which would cling to the leg and thus give the wearer better protection". Sometimes a cable pattern, a pattern on the sides, or a "quirk" (or clock) would ornament the stocking. The finished stockings were pressed beneath stocking boards with weights placed on top or they were placed on a stocking blocker, a wooden board in the shape of a stocking.

The stockings made for sale in the market were usually worked in plain Stockinette stitch with a ribbed top or welt. In Cardiganshire, the custom was to knit the top and toe in natural white yarn and the rest of the stocking in a dyed color. It was believed that natural-colored yarn wore better than dyed yarn and that the lanolin in the undyed yarn weatherproofed the stockings, which were often exposed at the tops of boots. This use of natural and colored yarn is evident throughout Britain.

The stockings made in rural Wales, like those made in Yorkshire, were sold at the village markets or purchased by hosiers, who bought up dozens of stockings to resell in London or other English towns. Sometimes Welsh cattle-drivers took stockings with them to sell on their journeys into England. Stockings were transported to the markets by the knitter, who frequently had to carry a heavy sack of stockings on her back for many miles from her home to the market town. When the stockings were sold, she would trudge back home, carrying the provisions purchased with her stocking earnings in the same manner.

HAND-KNITTING
IN THE CHANNEL ISLANDS

By the time Elizabeth I came to the throne, the knitting of fine wool stockings had become a big business. This new fashion of hand-knit stockings was a welcome addition to the industry of the Channel Islands.

In *The Fantastical Folly of Fashion*, Thirsk says that jersey stockings were a speciality of the islands of Jersey and Guernsey. The wool was combed and spun on a small Guernsey or Jersey spinning wheel. The secret of this worsted, spun, elastic, Stockinette-stitch fabric was discovered by other knitters, and by 1600, in Norwich alone, children earned £12,000 a year knitting these jersey stockings.

Wool for the fine stockings made on the Islands, as well as for waistcoats and other knitted items, was imported from England after the town of St. Peter Port obtained a royal license to do so in 1629. By the early seventeenth century, so many of the Islands' men, women, and children had taken up the trade of knitting that laws were necessary to keep them from knitting during harvest or vraic-cutting seasons. (Vraic is a seaweed used for fertilizer and fuel.) The Islands began to suffer for lack of laborers in the fields as even the strong and able-bodied were busy with their needles. Philip Dumaresq, in 1658, referred to knitting as the "lazy manufacture," although six thousand pairs of stockings were made each week; one pound of wool was required for three pairs (Rutt, *The History of Hand Knitting*).

In good weather, knitters would gather together under the trees for parties, called *veilles*, where they would sit in circles and socialize, knitting all the while. In winter, they met in each other's homes to prepare wool and knit, while chatter and merrymaking continued. These evenings were filled with rowdy songs and stories, and, of course, were a perfect place for couples to meet and for practical jokes to be played.

The knitters carried their week's work to markets in St. Helier or St. Peter Port. The stockings and other items made on the Islands were exported in great quantity to France, Spain and Italy. From early in the 1600s to the industry's decline at the end of the eighteenth century, the de Sausmarez family played a major role in the manufacture and export of handknitted goods. Family letters written in the late seventeenth century and cited by Rutt describe *bas à canon*, the type of stockings popular at the time: long, wide at the top, worn with breeches that were decorated with ribbons and laces. These stockings were no doubt expensive luxury apparel. Colors ranged from white to plum, gray-brown, or a bright reddish-brown. Many stockings were striped, either vertically or horizontally, with black and white, green and white, blue and white, or mottled colored yarns.

Rutt also reports that a Parisian merchant described the current fashion trends in a letter to one of the de Saus-

Stockings from the Shetland Island, Foula

marez: "The stripes must continue up the thigh (not half way up) and must be in bands of three: a black stripe between two narrow white ones; then a band of mottled yarn of a width equal to the three black and white stripes." Oddly, stockings for men and children were mentioned, but rarely stockings for women. Rhingraves, a type of breeches, decorated with ruffles and ribbons and probably worn with the *bas à canon*, were also manufactured during this time.

France provided the market for many of these knit items, and consequently when Jean-Baptist Colbert became the chief minister in 1661, the fortunes of the islanders began to change. To aid France's failing economy, Colbert placed restrictions and duties on imports of all kinds, which included knitted stockings, among other textiles. The knitted goods from the Channel Islands were now routed through England and then on to other countries.

Although the hand-knitting industry declined on the Channel Islands as it did elsewhere, the art of knitting remained with the people. Rutt also cites that in 1837, Edward Durrell noted about Jersey "This may be called the land of knitters: there is scarcely a female but who can knit. Strangers may remark it as a peculiar feature of the character of the people, to see females of the humbler classes knitting as they move leisurely along the lanes in the country. Not many years ago they might have been seen in that attire going on a Saturday to St Helier's market."

HAND-KNITTERS OF SCOTLAND

By the seventeenth century, knitting was widely practiced in the rural areas and towns of Scotland. In early times, the Scotsman, as did his Irish brother to the west, went barelegged. "The legs of these extraordinarily hardy men, through constant exposure to sun, wind, and rain, were permanently tanned to a deep red brown color which gained for them in Scotland the nickname of 'Redshanks'" (McClintock, *Old Irish and Highland Dress*).

Worn above these bare legs was the early Irish and Scottish loose-fitting tunic or shirt, often dyed a saffron color, and a cloak—garments quite unlike those worn by other Northern European people. In seventeenth-century Scotland, this style of dress was replaced by the belted *plaid* (Gaelic for blanket). This rectangle of fabric, six yards long and two yards wide, was placed on the ground, and folded in lengthwise pleats over a belt. The wearer would then lie on the fabric, wrap it around his body and fasten

the belt. The upper section served as protection from cold or stormy weather and the lower part served as a skirt, covering the legs. At night, the belt was undone and the plaid became a blanket to curl up in. In Gaelic, this garment was called a *féilidh mor*—great kilt. The *féilidh mor* was replaced by the simple *féilidh beag*, the skirt part of the garment. This "little kilt" was less cumbersome and eventually became the uniform of the Highland regiments. Long trousers, called *trews*, were worn mostly by the well off, in winter, or for riding, but they were not as common as the kilt. Trews and the little kilt were both made of tartan (brightly colored woven wool fabric).

The leg coverings worn with the kilt were leggings of cut-and-sewn woven fabric, usually linen. The hose, reaching to the knee and leaving the rest of the leg bare, was made with the same material as the kilt. In 1702, the Reverend Thomas Morer wrote that "Those who have stockings make 'em generally of the same piece with their plaids, not knitted or weaved, but sowd together and they tie them below the knee with tufted garters."

The Scots have been given credit for the invention of knitting due to the fact that in 1527 the cap knitter's of Paris chose St. Fiacra, reputedly the son of a Scottish king, as their patron saint. (St. Fiacra was actually an Irishman.) It is more likely, however, that knitting found its way to Scotland via the traders who visited Scottish ports or via English contacts. The English used knitting, as they did the ban on Highland dress after the battle of Culloden in 1746, to subdue the rebellious Scots. The English were fearful of the Scottish preference for hunting and herding and attempted to settle the Highland folk into "useful" occupations. Knitting was taught as a way to create docile and obedient subjects.

The knitters who lived near Aberdeen in the northeast of Scotland specialized in hand-knit stockings. In an article entitled "The Aberdeen Stocking Trade", Ishbel

Tartan Socks

Barnes reported that they worked mostly for export, and by 1743, had exported 219,360 pairs of stockings; by 1793, exports rose to a peak of 910,320 pairs of stockings.

The knitters, known as shankers, were usually women, but sometimes also old men and boys. The knitter was also frequently the spinner, and so would make more money. The use of the spinning wheel rather than the "rock and spindle", allowed the knitter to triple her output. A good knitter could finish two pairs of stockings a week if someone else spun the yarn for her. When the steel knitting needles were not in use, they were stored in a barrel of oatmeal to keep them from rusting.

Merchants from Aberdeen would visit the homes of the shankers and would often exchange wool in trade for the knitted stockings. The stockings were exported to ports far from Scotland, such as Bergen, Norway, Rotterdam, and Danzig (Gdansk). Traveling Scottish traders sold stockings throughout Europe.

The quality of the hand-knit stockings varied, and authorities struggled constantly to keep the goods to a minimum standard. Parliament stipulated in 1720 that "each pair of stockings made in Scotland for sale should be of one type of yarn and even workmanship throughout, free of such blatant faults as 'left loops, hanging hairs, and of burnt, cut or mended holes'" (Helen Bennett, *Scottish Knitting*).

Knitting stockings was an important part of the livelihood of both town dweller and crofter (farmer). Barnes reports that one landlord gave out wool to his tenants and received the stockings made from it as payment for rent. However, despite the work that knitting provided, some found fault. One minister complained that it allowed his parishioners to "associate with bad company of both sexes and tended to corrupt their morals". Another noted that, as knitting generally was carried on while people were seated, it was "too sedentary and unhealthy".

Cloth hose, cut and sewn from tartan, were the leg coverings preferred by the Highlanders and people of the Western Isles, even after knitting had taken hold elsewhere in Scotland. It wasn't until the nineteenth century that knitting gained a stronghold in these areas, due in part to a famine in 1846-1848, during which some landowners encouraged women to knit to supplement their meager incomes.

As a substitute for the cloth hose worn with the tartan kilt, the knitters developed Argyle patterning. Argyle stockings are made flat on two needles, and a separate ball of wool is used for each of the diamond-shaped pattern areas, which have lines of alternate color running through their centers. Hand-knitted tartan hose were often of two colors only, such as black and white or red and black. Argyle stockings were labor intensive to knit and therefore expensive. Plain hose with some patterning in the turndown tops and along the leg took the place of tartan hose for everyday wear.

As on the mainland, the crofters on the Islands were also able to add to their small incomes by knitting. Knitting was probably introduced to Shetland and Fair Isle, as in many other parts of Europe, in the sixteenth century. These islands, although remote, had been for centuries a crossroads for traders and seamen from the Baltic, Scandinavia, Europe, and beyond. These sailors brought goods from other lands to the islands, inspiring the knitters who lived there.

The people of the islands are a mix of Norse and Scottish blood, though they have been politically linked to Scotland since the 1200s. Traces of the Old Norn language still exist in many Shetland words, and many remnants of Nordic culture remain even today. Knitting, according to Rutt, probably came to the Islands from England via mainland Scotland, as the words in Shetland dialect that relate to knitting are not Norn but English.

As the skill developed, Shetlanders found a market for their wares in the sailors who fished the rich waters around the Islands. The visiting sailors came in droves and temporary housing was prepared for them each summer. Booths for trading were built along the quay-side in Lerwick (the main town on the Islands). These men from Germany, Holland, and other European countries traded cloth, tobacco, bread, brandy, or even money for the handknit stockings, caps, or gloves.

"By sea and land, everyone who could be spared from the crofts, old and young, excited as children on their way to a party, headed the same way. Women knitted as they walked, kishies on their backs filled with woolen stockings, caps, haps (shawls), and gloves. Barefoot boys led shaggy ponies almost hidden under bulging meshies (panniers) of butter, reistit mutton, salted beef, eggs, hens, and geese. Some threaded their way across the moor by way of the old broch of Clickhimin to the east Ness of Sound where their menfolk were busy cobbling together ramshackle huts, driftwood shelters, and rough canvas tents, while others from north and west gathered at the Hollanders' Knowe between Scalloway and Bressay Sound.

Fresh-faced, nubile country lasses, trigged out in their best, stronglegged and lissom, released from milking kye or raising peat, their backs yet unbent with delling the pitiless soil nor hips broadened with continual child-bearing, they chattered like starlings. The old, nodding in rusty black, heads decently covered, blinking in the bright sun, predicted with bitter wisdom that there would be 'mair heard o'this'. They had seen it all before but nothing would have kept them away and needles clacked in twisted hands even faster than their tongues" (Balneaves, *The Windswept Isles*).

Balneaves also reports that in 1614, the numbers of boats that came from foreign ports—such as Hoorne,

Schiedam, Rotterdam, and Katwijk—was over 1000, with a crew of 16 to 24 in the "great busses", of which there were 600. The rest were smaller tenders of different kinds. The law stated that no nets could be set prior to June 24, The Feast Day of St. John the Baptist, but the fleet left their home ports three weeks earlier in order to have time to trade or buy "fresh meat and provisions and for the hosiery for which the islands were already famous".

An example of the type of stocking knit at this time comes from the grave of a young man found at Gunnister on the island of Unst and recorded by the Society of Antiquaries of Scotland. He was buried in his clothes, and the Swedish and Dutch coins in his purse are dated around 1680. There were several pieces of knitting; two caps, gloves, a fragment, and his stockings. The stockings are 23 inches long with an 11-inch-long foot. The dark black-brown wool is two ply and was knitted at $7\frac{1}{2}$ stitches to the inch. There are clocks on both sides of the ankles, with a diamond pattern in moss stitch. The heel and foot are worn and had been repeatedly repaired. These stockings are similar in their shaping to the cut and sewn stockings worn prior to the popularity of knitted stockings.

Life was hard for these people. The island weather was inclement, and it was hard to make a living. The sea, while offering a livelihood by fishing, also took the lives of many fathers, husbands, and sons. Knitting or *makkin* provided a means of work through the long winter and, as in other parts of Britain, the knitters would gather to work around a peat fire, joining together in a social atmosphere. These *cairdins* were attended by old and young—some carding wool, some spinning and knitting—and there would be fiddle music and dancing after the work was done.

The harsh rule of the Scottish lairds added to the hardships of the people, as they were required to pay rents for the land they lived on. These rents took the form of part of the day's catch, potatoes from the croft, or finished knit-

Shetland Knitter

ting. As merchants began buying knitted items or trading goods for them, the knitters were further taken advantage of. The merchant would often pay only in his own goods, and so he got the knitted goods at a bargain price and made a double profit when he resold them. If the knitter asked for money instead, the merchant deducted twenty-five percent of the agreed value of the work. (Balneaves, *The Windswept Isles*)

Women knitted as they tended the sheep or walked with *kushies*, a type of basket, of peat on their backs. "The women of the skerries(off-shore islands) knit as they traveled to Whalsey or Lerwick and it was said that in foggy weather they could have a good idea of the distance sailed by the length of the knitting produced." (Nicolson, *Traditional Life in Shetland*) Not unlike the knitters of Wales, country women who had moved to town returned to their home region to visit and also *tigging for oo*, gathering up fleece from their friends and relations so they would have enough to keep busy spinning and knitting.

The hand knitting of stockings had succeeded in many rural areas because the work was portable and could be carried on in the midst of other chores or between seasonal jobs. The knitters could keep pace with hand spinners, and the price of hand labor made it much more lucrative for the merchants than purchasing expensive frames, creating workshops, and training skilled labor would have been.

The late 1700s marked the end of centuries of the hand-knitting stocking industry in Britain. The spinning wheel put out yarn at such a great rate that hand knitters could no longer keep up the production, and the hand knitter was gradually replaced by the stocking frame. Also, the Revolutionary War in America and the Napoleonic Wars in Europe led to upheavals in the market. Although hand-knit stockings were more durable than those made on a frame, they were generally not knit at as fine a gauge as the frame-knit stockings. The time it required to hand knit fine stockings made the price unreasonable, and the commercial value of machines and the steam to run them was beginning to outweigh the advantages offered by the craftsperson. Factories were a new idea, and the Industrial Revolution was at hand.

Even though mills on the Scottish mainland, in places like Brora and Inverness, took over the carding and spinning of wool, the Shetland women continued to hand knit the fine lace shawls and patterned jumpers which they continue to sell today.

FOUR

KNITTING IN OTHER EUROPEAN COUNTRIES

Traditions and stocking styles

It was not only in Britain but in many parts of Europe that hand knitting became a customary activity for common people. Knitting replaced the techniques of sprang and knotless netting, or nålbinding, for making close-fitting and elastic items for hand, head, and leg. Knotless netting is a much more time-consuming technique and requires a skilled and nimble hand to work. The contrast between the two techniques is well described in *History of Knitting Before Mass Production* which quoted the old Finnish saying "he who wears knitted mittens has an unskilled wife". Although the technique of knotless netting is still practiced today, in Nor-

Socks made with the nålbinding technique, fulled and unfulled.

way, Sweden, and other parts of Scandinavia as well as Iran, the strength and durability of the fabric were overshadowed by the advantages of knitted fabric: its elastic properties, versatility, suitability for complicated shapes such as the fingers of gloves and the heels of socks, speed of construction, and marketability.

THE FORMATION OF GUILDS

Much of the knitting was done by women for household use or by nuns for religious clothing, but because of the popularity and demand for knitted items, guilds of knitters, whose members were almost exclusively men, formed throughout western and central Europe. The guilds brought together workers in a type of trade union: to protect their wage-earning power, to resist increased production, to limit the number of journeymen and apprentices, and to protect them from competition from unskilled workers.

Throughout Europe, knitted items, particularly for personal use, varied from region to region.

In *History of Knitting Before Mass Production*, Irene Turnau gives us much of the history of these guilds. Statutes for the various knitter's guilds differed. To become a master knitter generally required an apprenticeship; in the Champagne region of France and the Upper Rhine region of Germany it was three years, in Rennes, France, the apprenticeship was five years. After the apprenticeship period was complete, some guilds required that the knitter become a journeyman, traveling and working for different masters; others allowed him to set up his own workshop.

Before the title of master was bestowed, however, the knitter had to produce a series of masterworks, depending on the various guild statutes. The guild statute from Vienna, 1609, lists a "table carpet in six colors, a beret, a pair of silk stockings, and a pair of gloves". As of 1605, a statute was in force in all the towns of Alsace and near the Swiss frontier—an area that also produced linen leggings and stockings. This statute, similar to the one in Prague, stated that a master was required to work a flower-patterned carpet, a cap, a woolen waistcoat, and gloves. The rules also stated that imperfections could not be covered up with chalk nor could wool from dead or butchered sheep be used. Guild members were forbidden to employ untrained servants but could employ their own children or other family members. The Viennese statute from 1689 states that the more complicated work, particularly the footpart of a stocking and repairs to knitwear should not be done by women servants. Masterworks often included stockings—riding stockings, wool and cotton stockings, red stockings, men's stockings from beaver hair, summer stockings with Spanish gussets, and fulled men's and ladies stockings.

Many of the products knitted under the guild system were fulled upon completion, either before or after dyeing. Fulling consisted of rinsing the knitted piece in an alkaline solution—stale urine, a type of clay called fuller's earth, or soap—to remove fat and dirt from the product. The fabric was then pounded with wooden mallets or fists, or trampled underfoot. This treatment would give the articles thickness and greater durability, and often disguised any loose stitches or other knitting errors. Fulling was done in the workshops, or less frequently and on a smaller scale, at home. The waste water resulting from fulling was a pollutant, so the location of these operations was regulated. Fulled garments were dried on wooden frames to give them shape and reduce shrinkage. They were also brushed when partially dried to raise the long hairs, which were then sheared with scissors. Knitted garments made of linen, silk and cotton were also dried on wooden forms.

Although the guilds were responsible for the more costly, "manufactured" products, much knitting was done in a domestic setting as part of a cottage industry. This was true particularly in the northern countries of Europe, on seacoasts, and in areas where the land was not the best for earning a living and where private production filled the needs of peasants and village dwellers. A Polish law from 1616 declared: "Peasants are prohibited from wearing knitted stockings (that are purchased) and permitted to wear only woolen ones which they themselves can make and dye." As in Britain, most of the finished goods were taken to market in a basket and sold to add income to the family purse.

Stockings became a part of common dress for almost all people throughout Europe. Knitted stockings appeared in Russia by 1630. According to Irene Turnau, "knitted stockings belonged among luxurious imports in the seventeenth century . . . in 1642, Tsarina Yevdokya owned three pairs of silk stockings embroidered with gold threads, labeled as 'German' stockings". That a member of the elite possessed only three pairs of stockings gives an idea as to their availability.

In 1700, Tsar Peter I ordered all members of the population who had any contact with his court to change their dress to styles inspired by Western Europe. This meant men had to shave their long beards and wear breeches and stockings rather than the traditional long robes. Wearing a beard resulted in heavy taxation, and the Tsar took the liberty of personally shaving his nobles. Tailors were forbidden to make traditional Russian clothes, and merchants were threatened with imprisonment for selling them. Even the soldiers were fitted with uniforms based on Western European styles, which included stockings.

Stockings and hose were often made of cut and sewn cloth, quilted or lined with fur. For warmth, wearing sev-

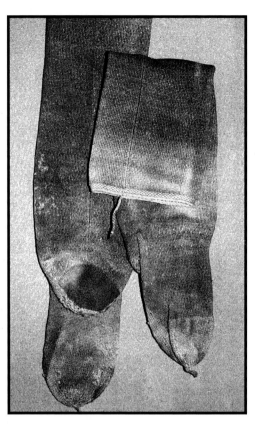

2-ended stockings of red-dyed wool. Stockings have wadmal on heels.

eral pairs of stockings or wrapping the feet with rags or cloth was common practice, not only in Russia, but in Poland, the Ukraine, and elsewhere.

Throughout Europe, knitted items, particularly for personal use, varied from region to region. Patterns and colors were unique to certain areas. Much interesting ornamentation was devised to decorate gloves, mittens, and stockings. Stockinette stitch and garter stitch were common, as were geometric patterns worked in knit and purl stitches. Floral, geometric, and other figured designs were popular in the knitting of Scandinavia and the Baltic countries. Cut and sewn hose had a wedge inserted on the outside of the ankle, which was necessary to aid in the fit of the garment. When knitted stockings became popular, these wedges, called *svikler* in Danish and *zwickle* in German, were embroidered or embellished with decorative stitches.

The seacoasts, mountainous areas, and Nordic countries were prime knitting areas. Wool, of course, was the basic raw material for knitted goods, spun on a spindle or wheel. The work was done by older children and women primarily, with needles of wood, metal, or bone. The knitting sheath, or stick, was a tool found throughout Europe, from Holland to Portugal, in many variations.

With iron and brass

needles, they made

leggings, stockings without

feet as well as stockings

with feet. The men knit the

legs and the girls made the

heels.

Red and white mottled-wool yarn sock from Sweden.

Some of the oldest existing knitted garments have been found in Denmark. By the 1600s, near Herning in Jutland, there was a large market for the manufacture of hand-knitted stockings.

The land in mid-Jutland was better suited to sheep raising than farming. Young and old, male and female knitted as they plowed, herded the animals, walked, or rode. Knitters would come together for a *bindestue*, or knitting bee, where they told stories, sang, and discussed the events of the day. With iron and brass needles, they made leggings called *stunthoser*, stomper, or stockings without feet, as well as stockings with feet. The men knit the legs and the women and girls made the heels. The stockings were often of one color, knitted loosely and slightly fulled in warm water or fish broth. Many of these items were sold to merchants who traded their wares elsewhere in Denmark, Germany, America, and other countries.

Records dating from the 1700s that are cited in the Danish book *Bondestrik* indicate that in the area around Århus, women's stockings were blue, black, white, or a blue-and-white plied mix. In some cases, if two colors were plied together, the white strand was linen. Linen, silk, and camel-hair stockings were also knit. Red woolen stockings, heavily fulled with clocked ankles, were possibly part of a bride's costume. An ikat-like dyed yarn, called flame yarn, was a mixture of shades of one color and was used for stockings throughout Scandinavia. Cotton stockings became popular in the late 1800s, decorated with fancy borders, seams, clocks, and lace patterns. *Ringede* stockings, also called *klingelhoser*, with horizontal stripes, were common all over Denmark as children's stockings and also bride's stockings. The color combinations varied: red and blue, red and violet, red and gray, or gray and blue. Most of the men's stockings were white or dark blue.

Danish stockings were knit both in thick and thin yarns; some were fulled, some were not. Everyday stockings were plain, with only a ribbed border at the top. Stockings for festive days were more decorative, with a back "seam", and embellished at the ankle with clocks worked in purl stitches, or designs worked in traveling stitches, single stitches that pass over or under the stitch next to it to move across the surface of the fabric. The patterned stockings from Hedebo and Falster were especially decorative, with vertical purl stripes, angled stripes, and squares and triangles in purl stitches.

STOCKINGS IN SWEDEN

The need for warm, dry feet led to great inventiveness on the part of the peasant farmers and timbermen of northern Sweden. As late as the second half of the nineteenth century, leg coverings were still made of woven linen cloth or of *wadmal*, a thick, fulled and napped woolen cloth. The linen hose was not shaped, but rather resembled a tube without a foot. The foot was protected in various ways; by a knitted sock, hay stuffed in the shoe or boot, strips of cloth wrapped around the foot (as in the early Middle Ages), an insole lining the shoe, or a cap, probably nålbinded, worn over the toe. "Long socks", similar to medieval hose, or "snow socks" worn over the shoes were also used.

Stockings were commonly knit in a twined, or two-end, technique, in which two ends, usually from the same ball of yarn, are knit into one piece. A stitch is worked with each end, alternating one after the other. The resulting fabric looks like common knitted fabric, but is thicker and less elastic, although very sturdy and warm.

Single-color stockings were dyed red or blue. The foot was usually not dyed, in order to conserve the precious dye, and also because lanolin in the natural, undyed wool made it warmer and more durable than the dyed wool. Sometimes two colors of yarn were used—natural white and natural black. The finished article was then usually dyed, red being the most common color. If the article had been worked in two colors, the white areas turned red, and the black remained black. By the seventeenth century, when knitted stockings became part of daily dress, natural colors were more common; colored stockings were worn on special occasions. In the mid-1800s, horizontal- or vertical-striped stockings and cotton stockings with lace patterns were the fashion of the day, not only in Sweden but throughout Europe.

Horse hair, cow hair and tail bristles, goat hair, and even women's hair were often mixed with the wool as it was spun into yarn. Yarn made with a mixture of wool and hair is more water repellent and therefore good for insoles, the heels and feet of stockings, and for mittens and gloves.

The twined-knit stockings from these northern regions, especially Sweden, frequently had a baggy shape and fitted loosely, patterned after the cloth hose that were also still in use. They often had a seam down the back of the leg, known as a "hair" in the village of Dala-Floda, and a dart- or wedge-shaped clock along the calf (Nylén, *Swedish Handcraft*). Both the seam and the side dart reflect the influence of cloth hose on the styling of knit stockings. The fulling of knit stockings also created a fabric similar to *wadmal*.

By the mid-1700s, the Halland region of southern Sweden was a major center for knitting as decentralized industry—industry in the home rather than a factory or central workplace, known as the putting-out system. The people of Våxtrop, Hök, and Hasslöv earned much of their livelihood knitting thick woolen stockings. A large fair was held in Våxtrop twice a year, and stockings from surrounding parishes were brought to market and sold there.

By the 1770s, Halland was known for its women's stockings with colored gussets. In Skåne, also a southern region, bridegroom's stockings were white wool, beautifully patterned in knit and purl stitches. In contrast, women's wedding stockings were plain and of black wool. Openwork-patterned, white cotton stockings were also made in this region. Similar stockings were made in other parts of southern Sweden, with traditions spreading between older styles, cotton openwork or lace patterns, and colorwork patterns popular in the nineteenth century.

STOCKINGS IN NORWAY

Knitting found its way to Norway in much the same manner that it did to other northern countries.

In very early times, trading was conducted by fearless men who braved the open seas in small boats, traveling along wild coastlines and riverways to sell or barter goods to people living near natural harbors. These sailor-merchants formed associations, or *hansas*, to protect their rights on foreign lands and seas. The Hanseatic League eventually had great influence from Estonia to Edinburgh, organizing trade routes and operating great merchant houses. As people sold and bartered their crafts and produce to the traders, the harbor communities grew into villages. The villages eventually became populated with craftsmen and merchants, and grew into rich and prosperous cities, such as Riga in Latvia, Lubeck in Germany, and Visby on Gotland, an island in the Baltic between Sweden and Finland.

Bergen, Norway, was one of the Hanseatic towns, and many goods were imported to and exported from there—not the least of which was the humble sock, unloaded in bales upon the quay side. A knit woolen fragment dating from around 1500 has been unearthed in Bergen, and may have been made there or imported.

Knitting was mostly woman's work in Norway. In early times, it was associated with the lower classes—the poor and thieves. A story told in Kjellberg's *Strikking i Norge* is

*Norweigan
red mottled
stockings*

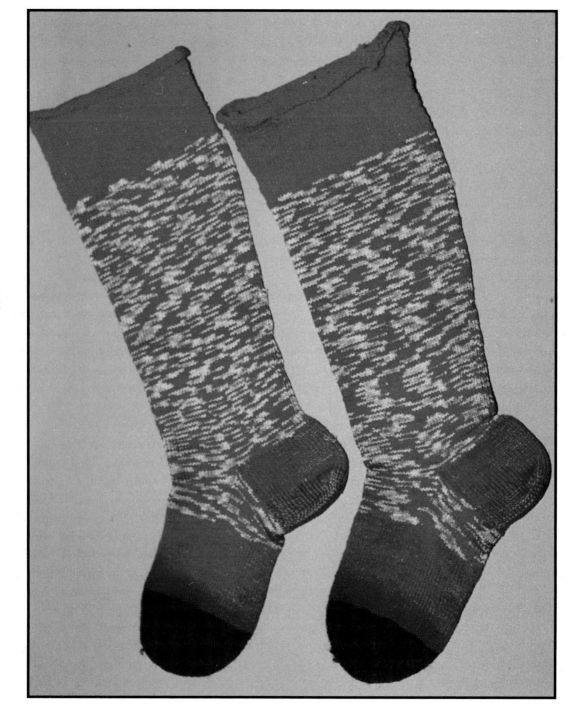

of a knitter named Lisbeth Pedersdatter, a vagabond who was arrested in 1634 along with her employer, Karen Eriksdatter, also a vagabond. Karen was accused of stealing garments and Lisbeth, whose crime was more serious, was accused of being a troll or a witch. The court documents state that Karen had taken Lisbeth into her service for one year and that her job was to carry her possessions and to knit stockings. It is likely that the stockings were not only for Karen but also for sale. As in many other places, knitting was an activity that women could make money at.

The early stockings knit in Norway were of coarse wool, often blended with cow or goat hair for added strength; the feet were sometimes covered with a sole of *wadmal*. Footless leggings, with straps under the foot, were also worn—the long style was known as *utapåhoser* and the short as *tålabber*.

Around 1800, white fancy stockings were decorated with embroidered eight-petaled rose designs along the ankle. Sometimes these designs were knitted into the stockings in a contrasting color or were worked in a combination of purl and knit stitches in a single color. Krotasåkka was another special design, made up of intricate knit and purl patterns and tiny cabled stitches. These decorative stockings were knit with white yarn; the women's were then dyed black.

Evidence of old Norwegian stockings with horizontal stripes of the same or different widths and in two or three colors have also been found. As shown in *Strikking i Norge*, sometimes the ribbing at the top of the leg, the heel, and the toe were worked with white yarn, and the leg and foot in colored yarn. Flame yarn (*flammegarn*) was also common in Norway. "The stockings were made out of homespun yarn that was made from the finest wool. It was first colored bright red, then strips of birch bark were wrapped very tightly around each skein of yarn at regular intervals. The skeins were then boiled in a brine of Brazil tree bark.

This made the yarn brown with bright red speckles . . . . Many pairs of these stockings have been preserved and the color combinations vary" (*Strikking i Norge*). There's another example of a flame yarn dyed blue, and then after the bark was removed, dyed red—the blue areas darkened and the white areas turned red. Men's stockings were usually simply blue and white.

STOCKINGS IN ICELAND AND THE FAEROE ISLANDS

Knitting arrived in Iceland with English, Dutch, and German traders. The earliest references to knitting, confirmed by the first Icelandic bible and reported by Pagoldh in *Nordic Knitting*, dates from 1584.

People of all ages and both sexes knit at home not only for their own use but for exportation of their goods as well. Pagoldh reports that in 1624, 72,000 pairs of stockings and more than 12,000 pairs of mittens were exported. Children learned to knit, spin, and read at four years of age, and a housemaid was expected to knit a pair of long stockings a day. The Icelanders made many types of knitted items, including stockings, socks and knitted insoles for shoes. The knitting was done with wool in natural colors, and the finished pieces were often heavily fulled.

The Faeroe Islands, part of Denmark, but Iceland's close neighbor to the southeast, also has a long history of knitting. The Norsemen who settled on the Faeroe Islands in the ninth century found a breed of small wild sheep. These sheep provided the beginnings of the woolen market for the Islanders. Woolen goods, which by the end of the 1500s were being exported to Norway, were traded for wood for houses and boats as well as other items. By 1765, according to Pagoldh, more than 100,000 pairs of stockings were exported. One can readily understand why sheep's wool was thought of as Faroese gold.

The Islanders also knit for their own use. They wore footless leggings called *leggold* with short, fulled, double-knitted slipperlike socks called *skóleistur*. Fishermen, often away on the seas for months, wore knitted over-the-knee stockings called *pulshosur*.

STOCKINGS IN FINLAND

As early as 1500, Birgittine nuns in the Finnish convent at Nådendal were making stockings and mittens, although these items may have been made with nålbinding rather than knitting. By the seventeenth century, knit stockings were being exported from Nådendal. By the next century, the city became known as a stocking city, and most of the men, women and children were involved in some form of knitting production. According to Pagoldh, knitting was so prevalent that the city officials had to ban knitting in public places as it was considered shameful.

A family's wealth and the worth of a bride was often judged by the quality and quantity of textiles, sheets, towels, and clothing, including knit stockings and mittens. These items were displayed in the summer sleeping lofts so that the prospective suitor, when he paid his evening visit, would be able to see what treasures his sweetheart's dowry contained. It was normal for a bride to have knit enough stockings to last for twenty years, or maybe her lifetime.

Although stockings were common clothing in Finland by the 1700s, people also wore leggings called *benholkar*. Before knitting had become popular, these had been made from woven fabric. The leggings were worn with shoes that were stuffed with hay or with birch-bark shoes, both impractical to wear with stockinged feet. Cotton and linen leggings were worn during the warmer times of the year. Some leggings began as stockings—when the stocking foot was worn out, it was cut off and the leg was used as a legging.

A family's wealth and the worth of a bride was often judged by the quality and quantity of textiles, … including knit stockings and mittens.

The colors of Finnish knitting were stronger and brighter than elsewhere in the northern lands, reflecting an Eastern influence. Patterns on stocking legs would be checkered or of scroll or zig-zag striped designs. Basketweave or entralac patterning was also popular. By the nineteenth century, when knitting with cotton became popular, stockings were made either in solid white (these could have also been made of linen) or with stripes of red and white on the leg, as mentioned in *Nordic Knitting*. In Osterbotten, stockings were made with long sheep's wool from the fall clipping, and were usually fulled and blocked on boards.

STOCKINGS IN ESTONIA AND LATVIA

Many of the knitting traditions of the Nordic countries are found in those of their Baltic neighbors to the south. The countries of Estonia, Latvia, and Lithuania were, from early times, a bridge between east and west, when baltic amber was traded to the Mediterranean lands in the time of the Romans. Later the Hanseatic merchants helped to create cities and ports along the coast.

In Estonia, knitting has always had an honorable place. Traditionally, gloves, mittens, jackets, lacy shawls, caps, and, of course, stockings, were hand-knit. The oldest examples of Estonian knitting—pieces of gloves and stockings—date from the last half of the seventeenth century and contain two-color pattern knitting. Prior to this time, foot and hand coverings were made with nålbinding or feet were wrapped with cloth bandages or protected with foot cloths.

Latvian woven belts

In Estonia, as in Finland, knitting played a part in courtship and wedding engagements. Tedre, in *Estonian Customs and Traditions* says that prior to the acceptance of the suitor, a member of his family, usually his mother or an elderly woman, would visit the potential bride and her family. The woman would present a bottle of spirits as a gift. If the bottle was returned to the suitor full, he had to keep looking for a wife. If it was returned empty but with a pair of mittens or socks tied with a garter or belt, he had been accepted.

By the day of her wedding, an Estonian bride had a dowry chest filled with stockings and mittens. A girl would start making many of the items for her dowry chest when she was young. Serious work would start after the engagement had been made, and the first banns were read. To help fill the chest, the bride would go gift or alms hunting, a custom known as "chasing the wolf's tail". The bride would offer wine to people, who would in turn give her wool, sometimes flax, and, in later times, finished stockings and mittens. At this point, friends and family would help out with the knitting.

On the day of the wedding, the bride would give many pairs of stockings and mittens, as well as woven belts, to the bridegroom, his family, and other participants in the festivities—such as the groom's men and bride's ladies, the musicians and officials. Wedding celebrations lasted three days or more, and the knitted gifts were usually presented on the morning after the first night the couple spent in their new home. These gifts were displayed to all the guests, and therefore much care was taken to make them special. The giving of these gifts was accompanied by the singing of a ritual song.

Along with the stockings, narrow blue or red bands or ribbons were also presented, usually handwoven on a small loom or rigid heddle loom. These ribbons were used as garters—tied under the knee of stockings with the ends hanging down as a fringe. The patterns were often similar to the patterns knit into the stockings.

Konsin, in *Slimkoeesemed* reports that stockings also played an important role in other significant rituals. Older women knit their funeral stockings and the stockings that were given to the gravedigger and the officials at the funeral. On June 24, St. John's Day, in the district of Vastseluna, white stockings were placed on the holy St. John rock as an offering. During sowing time in the district of Halliste, stockings were worn inside-out to trick the "evil one" and prevent him from harming the new plants. If a person lost his way, it was believed that all that was necessary to find the right path was for the wearer to turn his hat and stockings around.

Men's stockings were usually white, gray, natural black, or pot blue (a color dyed with indigo). In the area of Se-

Sock from Tarvastu

These ribbons were

used as garters—

tied under the knee

of the stockings

with the ends hanging

down as a fringe.

Young man from Pärnumaa, mid
19th century.

tumaa, however, men wore more colorful stockings with stripes and patterns. Women's stockings for everyday wear were white, red, blue, gray, or black. Red was common on the islands of Saaremaa and Hiiumaa off the Estonian coast, probably due to Swedish influence. Leggings were also worn by women in Estonia. Because stockings wore out faster, leggings were more practical. They were worn in winter for warmth and in summer to protect women's legs from their heavy woolen skirts. When they wore linen skirts, they went bare-legged.

In other districts, geometric designs in cobalt blue, greenish yellow, and brownish red were knit on a white background. Many of the pattern designs used in knit stockings are also found in mittens. Some of the most common were moon, butterfly, fish tail, cat's paw, sheep eye, strawberry leaf, table leg, pine, and sieve. At the end of the nineteenth century, figures of animals and people appeared.

Many of the different regions of the country had their own typical decorative patterns, often with geometric bands of patterning quite similar to those found in Fair Isle or Shetland knitting. These banded stockings often had patterned clock decorations at the ankles. Many patterned bands were centered at the calf area rather than at the top or all the way along the leg, and some were very wide. These wide bands were desirable because a woman's heavy calves were a sign of her strength and good health. She would pad her calves with fabric and then pull the stockings over the padding.

The most colorful and patterned stockings came from the islands of Kihnu and Muhu. These were usually for women's use on festival days or special occasions. They had patterned bands around the top of the stocking, with white or light-colored legs and feet. The legs were often decorated with clocks (vikli) of twisted traveling stitches and purl stitches on a stockinette background.

Natural-colored stockings were decorated with embroidered or inlaid colors in roositid, or rose-patterned designs. These patterns were applied to the sides of the stockings above the ankles and often ran along the foot and heel in the same manner as the knitted clock designs. Natural-colored yarn was also used for lacy patterned stockings, much like the stockings popular in other European countries in the nineteenth and early twentieth centuries. Some Estonian stockings were knit in stripes of colors and flame yarns.

Many of the traditions of knitting in Estonia are also found in Latvia. Specific knitted patterns represent ancient symbols in life. Mara, God's helper, represented by a zig-zag design, protects all cattle and water and is involved with birth and death. Laimma, depicted by an arrow-point pattern, controls destiny. The use of certain patterns or colors also provided information about the district the wearers were from and their status in life (Lizbeth Upitis, Latvian Mitten Book).

A Latvian maiden could prove her worth by the amount and quality of knitting she produced. Although mittens were the most abundant of these items, stockings were also important. Mittens and sturdy socks called "brass" were given to the suitor as a sign of his acceptance.

As in Estonia, at the wedding festivities, the bride passed out mittens, stockings, and other items to those who helped with the ceremony and to her new family, who would wait with great expectation to see what treasures her dowry chest held. The bride would then be taken on a tour of her new home and she would offer knitted mittens and stockings at each important place—the sheep pen, the cow-byre, the hearth, the fruit trees, and the beehive. These gifts were symbolic wishes for a prosperous future life. The new mother-in-law later gathered up all these items.

Estonian Stockings

CARRYING ON THE TRADITION

How to knit a sock

❧

Knitting traditions, from the making of the Welsh farmer's stocking to an Estonian girl's colorful hose, developed as the result of both necessity and fashion. The need to have warm and protected feet led to the wrappings and bindings of early times. The spread of the craft of knitting enabled people to make stockings that fit and offered protection at the same time. It was men's fashion that first took advantage of the art of knitting with the development of long hose with embroidered patterns and stockings decorated with ornate clocks or knitted lace. Eventually, fashion put men's stockings in the place where they generally reside today—safely tucked away under a pair of trouser legs, peeking out at odd times. Ladies, on the other hand, wore their beautiful stockings hidden beneath long gowns until the twentieth century, when skirt lengths went up. In modern times, the wearing of no stockings at all is common. Girls in short skirts with bare legs are the redshanks of our time.

In spite of the great strides of technology—from William Lee's early knitting machine to the later manufactories of ready-made knitwear—the making of stockings by hand still holds an interest for knitters. There's an attraction to making a useful item with one's own hands. A hand-knit pair of stockings requires techniques that have been developed through history and talents that have been passed on from one knitter to the next. The knitting of stockings or socks provides a connection to history and each pair is, perhaps, a small honor to all the knitters who have had the great pleasure of creating a well-turned heel.

ESSENTIAL TECHNIQUES

The structural design of knitted socks and stockings has changed very little from when they were first knit centuries ago. Then, as now, the logical way to make a knitted article that covers part of the leg and the foot is to connect two tubes at an angle—one tube with an open end; the other with a closed end. Part of the art and the pleasure of knitting socks centers around the area where the two tubes connect, known as the heel.

The very first knitted stockings or socks were probably made on single-point needles and seamed. They may not have had shaped heels or toes and probably didn't fit very well. Double-point needles allow stockings and socks, as well as other garments, to be worked without seams. They were common by the fourteenth century. In the painting by Master Bertram for the Buxtehude Convent dating from just before 1400, Mary is knitting a circular garment on double-point needles, while the Christ Child plays at her feet.

Today, 600 years later, no better way has been invented to make hand-knit stockings. Oh sure, machines can do it quicker and cheaper, but there is something about the quality of a hand-knit sock that surpasses even the best that modern technology can offer. Double-point needles are truly a knitter's connection to history, and learning to use them is an achievement in itself. It isn't difficult, but it may look overwhelming at first.

In Europe, the tradition is to use four double-point needles to carry the stitches and a fifth to do the work. In Britain and the U.S., three needles are generally used to carry the stitches, with the fourth doing the work. Most of the directions given in this book are for a set of four needles—three to carry the stitches and one to use as a working needle. If you prefer to use a set of five needles, however, you can divide the instep stitches onto two needles.

There are numerous tips and special considerations for working various parts of the sock. In the next chapter you will find instructions for a classic sock. But first, let's look at the basic techniques required.

There are several good ways to cast on for socks. One is the Continental or Long-Tail Cast-On and the other is the English Cast-On, in two versions.

CONTINENTAL OR LONG-TAIL CAST-ON

This method of casting on creates a firm, elastic edge. You need only one needle to work this cast-on.

Make a slip knot and place it on the right-hand needle, leaving a long tail (leave enough length for the number of stitches you'll need to cast on for your sock size). Place the thumb and index finger of your left hand between the two threads. Secure the long ends with your other three fingers. Twist your wrist up so that your palm faces upward, and spread your thumb and index finger apart to make a V of the yarn around them.

Insert the needle into the yarn around your thumb, from front to back. Place the needle over the yarn around your index finger and bring the needle down through the loop around your thumb. Drop the loop off your thumb and, placing your thumb back in the V configuration, tight-

Continental Cast-On

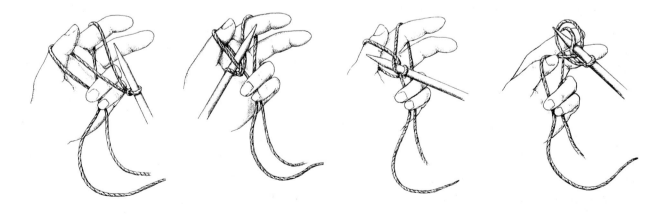

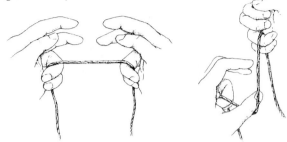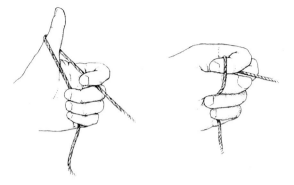

en up the resulting stitch on the needle. Repeat this process until all the stitches are cast on.

THE ENGLISH CAST-ON #1

This cast-on is very elastic. You will need one needle to work this cast-on. The extra twist in the initial loops creates a firm, solid edge that resembles purl stitches.

Hold the yarn between the middle and ring fingers of both hands with the end connected to the ball in the right hand. Push the thumb of your left hand down onto the yarn between your hands. With the index finger of your left hand, come over the top of the yarn around your thumb and hook the yarn around this finger. The loop on your index finger is the first stitch you will work. With your right hand, place the needle into the loop on your index finger and wrap the yarn in your right hand around the needle, and knit this stitch. Repeat this process until you have the desired number of stitches.

ENGLISH CAST-ON #2

This second method of English Cast-On is technically very similar to the Continental Cast-On. You need one needle to work this cast-on. (Paired with the Continental or Long-Tail Cast-On, this cast-on can be used to create a k1,p1 or k2,p2 cast-on edge.) A Continental Cast-On will give a knit stitch as a base. The English Cast-On will give a purl stitch as a base.

Make a slip knot and place it on the needle in your right hand, leaving a long tail (again, the length depends on the number of stitches you need to cast on). Place the thumb and index finger of your left hand between the two threads, and secure the long ends by closing your other three fingers on them. Twist your wrist up so that your palm points upward, and spread your thumb and index finger apart to make a V of the yarn around them. So far, this is just like the Continental Cast-On.

Place the needle in front of the yarn around your thumb and bring it underneath both threads around your thumb. Insert the needle down into the center of the loop around your thumb and bring the needle forward toward you. The loop around your thumb will have a twist in it, close to the needle. Now place the needle over the top of the yarn around your index finger, catch this yarn and insert the needle back down into the loop around your thumb. As you do this, turn your thumb slightly to remove the twist in the loop so as to allow the needle to pass through the untwisted loop. Drop the loop off your thumb, and placing your thumb back in the V configuration, tighten up the resulting stitch on the needle. Repeat this process until all the stitches are cast on.

Using one of these techniques, cast on the necessary number of stitches onto one of your double-point needles. Count them again to be sure you have the correct number. Distribute these stitches onto three needles by slip-

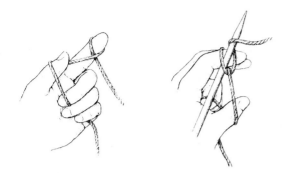

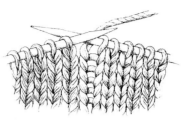

Line of loose stitches

ping them, one at a time as if to purl, onto the empty needles. When one third of the stitches are on one of these needles, slip the next third of the stitches onto another empty needle. After you fill up the first needle, it is handy to stick the point of it into your ball or skein of yarn to keep this first needle stationary while you move the next group of stitches.

After your stitches are distributed on your needles, count them and shift them if necessary so that you have an even number on each needle. You might not have the same number of stitches on each needle. For instance, if you cast on 64 stitches, your three needles should have 20, 22 and 22 stitches, respectively. This makes it easier to work a k1,p1 ribbing as the first stitch of each needle will be a knit stitch and the last stitch of each needle will be a purl stitch. You will have a neater transition working a purl at the end of one needle and a knit at the beginning of the next needle. Because you are working circularly, a loose stitch at this transition point becomes a noticeable

line down the leg of your stocking—potentially in three or four places! Another way to alleviate this problem is to move your stitches around on the needles from time to time as you are working the leg. That way, the loose stitch won't always be in the same place, and the line will be less noticeable. If you do this, you may want to place a marker at the beginning of your round.

(If you are working with a set of five needles instead of four, divide your stitches into fourths instead of thirds, as evenly as possible.)

Notes and special considerations:

The cast-on row for a sock must be strong and even, as it may be visible. It must also be elastic, so that the sock will stretch when pulled on over the foot and will stay up while it's being worn. If you tend to cast on tightly, use a needle one size larger for casting on than you will use to knit the sock, or try casting onto two needles held together of the size the sock will be worked with.

English Cast-On #2

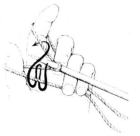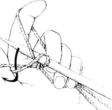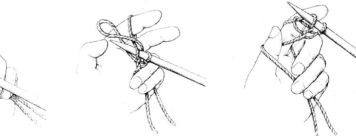

The following decreases are interchangeable. Pick one you like and use it consistently in one area of a sock. For example, use one decrease in turning the heel and another when decreasing for the heel gusset, but keep all the decreases in an area the same. This gives a nicer finish to the sock. All of these decreases will produce stitches that lie to the left with the exception of K2 tog, which is a right-leaning decrease. Use left-leaning decreases as you begin a group of stitches or at the beginning of a needle.

SSK: Slip, slip, knit. Slip one as if to knit, slip one as if to knit, insert the needle into the front of these two slipped stitches with the left needle from left to right and knit them together.

An SSK can also be worked by slipping one as if to knit, slipping one as if to purl and then knitting the two slipped stitches together as above.

Sl1, k1, PSSO: Slip one, knit one, pass slipped stitch over. Slip one stitch as if to knit, knit one stitch, pass the slipped stitch over the knit stitch, and drop it off the needle.

K2 tog tbl: Knit two together through the back loops.

Use a right-leaning decrease as you end a needle or group of stitches, as at the end of needle #1 in the gusset shaping.

K2 tog: Knit two together.

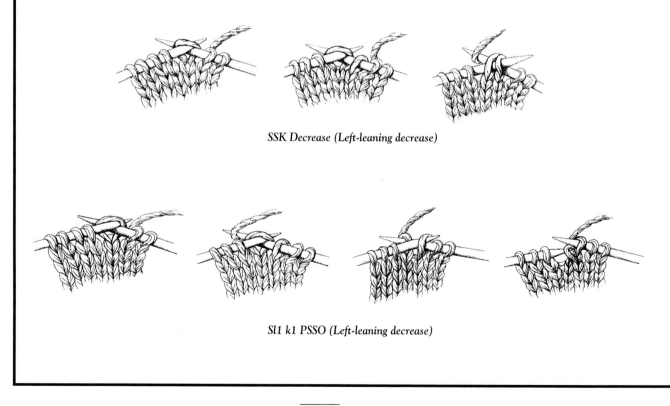

SSK Decrease (Left-leaning decrease)

Sl1 k1 PSSO (Left-leaning decrease)

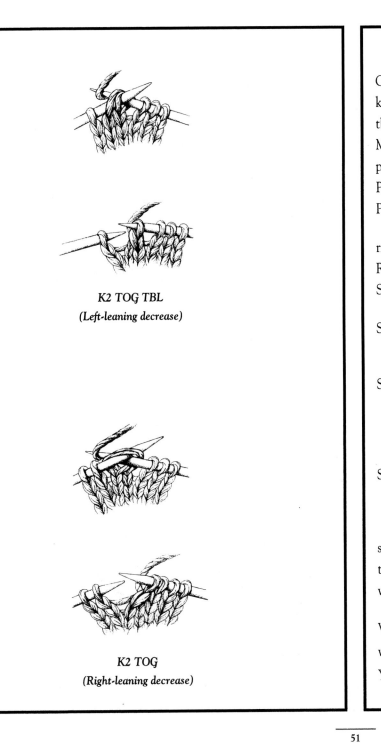

K2 TOG TBL
(Left-leaning decrease)

K2 TOG
(Right-leaning decrease)

CO	Cast on
k	Knit
tbl	Through the back loop.
M	Marker
p	Purl
PSSO	Pass slipped stitch over.
P2SS	Pass two slipped stitches over at the same time.
rnd(s)	round(s)
RS	Right side
Sl1	Slip one stitch as if to purl unless otherwise stated.
SSK	Slip one stitch as if to knit, slip another stitch as if to knit, then knit these two stitches together.
SSP	Slip one stitch as if to purl, slip another stitch as if to purl, then go into the back of the two stitches with the left-hand needle and purl the two stitches together.
St st	Stockinette stitch. Knit every round when working circularly. Knit one row, purl one row when working back and forth.
st(s)	Stitch(es)
tog	Together
work even	Work in established pattern without increasing or decreasing
WS	Wrong side
wyf	With yarn in front
YO	Wrap yarn over needle

In the long tradition of the cottage-industry knitters, the guild knitters, and even knitting teachers in nineteenth-century schools, sock measurements are based on proportions. Some of the traditional rules of knitting stockings or socks can certainly be applied to modern knitting, as the way we knit a sock today is no different from the way a sock was knit three hundred years ago. These rules of thumb for measurement are interesting and, while not set in stone, give stocking knitters a point from which to begin their plans and a way to keep track as they're working.

In her book, Mary Thomas, attributes her knowledge of measurement to "Granny". She records that the length of a leg for long stockings—those that come above the knee—should measure three times the length of the wearer's foot. To shape this long stocking, it is necessary to work twice the length of the foot before beginning the decreases along the leg. Long stockings usually have a 1-inch hem or ribbing.

The length of the leg of golf hose, stockings worn with knickerbockers, kilt hose, or knee stockings should measure two times the length of the foot. This measurement is taken from below the traditional turned-down top. The turned-down top measures 3 to 4 inches, and the ribbing that hides beneath it, which acts as a sort of garter to help hold the stocking up, is generally 2 inches long.

According to Granny, socks, on the other hand, were to have a 4-to 5-inch ribbing for adults and a 1½-inch ribbing for children. The rest of the leg should be the same length as the wearer's foot.

The Danish book *Bondestrick* contains some wonderful rules for measuring the foot of a sock or stocking. According to this source, the length of the knitted foot is correct if the heel and toe meet when wrapped around the wearer's fist. After conducting some research, I found that this rule proves true almost every time. Another rule—a variation on the previous one—advises the knitter to begin toe decreases when the foot of the stocking in progress is laid around the flat palm of the wearer's hand and the needles meet the heel. This rule is a handy one—it saves you from chasing down a measuring tape as you frantically work to arrive at the toe.

A knitting needle is also a convenient way of measuring. Double-point needles are generally 7 inches or 8 inches long, although some are shorter or longer. If you know the length of your needle, you can use it as a guide as you knit a leg or as a way to approximate the foot measurement. It may require a bit of guesswork, but you will have a close measurement.

Before you begin to knit a sock, it's necessary to take actual measurements. You need to know the length of the wearer's foot from the back of the heel to the end of the toes, the ankle width and the desired height of the leg of the sock. It is also helpful to know the ankle height from the top of the ankle bone to the bottom of the heel. If the sock has an elastic fabric for the leg, like k2,p2 ribbing, it is not necessary to shape the leg. If the sock will be long with a ribbed cuff and a Stockinette-stitch leg, plan on decreasing several pairs of stitches, in intervals, down the center of the back of the leg. (Cast on six or eight extra stitches than necessary for the ankle so you'll have stitches to decrease.)

In planning a knee-length stocking, such as Norwegian type stockings or kilt hose, measure around the widest part of the calf. Also measure the ankle and the widest part of the foot, as well as the other measurements listed above. Multiply the inch measurement you have taken for the widest part of the leg by your gauge and then deduct twenty-five to thirty percent of that number. This will be the number of stitches to cast on, adjusted, of course, with pattern repeats in mind. This percentage reduction is necessary to make the stocking tighter than the actual leg measurement at the top, so that it will stay up. You don't want your stockings to fall down!

Now that the stitches are distributed onto your needles, you need to join your work. Be careful that all the stitches lie smoothly on the needles and are not twisted. Turn your set of needles with points facing up so that the needle with the first cast-on stitch is in your left hand and the needle with the last cast-on stitch and the yarn attached to the ball is in your right hand. Insert an empty needle into the first cast-on stitch—the one at the point of your left-hand needle—and knit, carrying the yarn across the gap from the point of the needle in your right hand. Tighten the working yarn to close the gap.

This "gap" is the area where the join occurs. By joining the round, you create an imperceptibly spiralling fabric. One row spirals into the next as you work around. The join often appears as a jag in the top edge of your sock. It can be hidden by the skillful weaving in of the tail that remains from casting on when the sock is finished, or you can make the join less obvious as you begin to knit. Do this by casting on one more stitch than intended for the sock leg and, before joining your work into a round, slip this extra stitch onto the left-hand needle, next to the first cast-on stitch. Now, when you join the round, knit together these first two stitches. This will give you the correct stitch count and also neaten up the joining place.

Another way to join circular knitting is to switch the positions of the first and last cast-on stitches prior to the start of knitting the round. Place the first stitch that was cast on onto the right-hand needle; then pass the last stitch that was cast on over the stitch you just moved, and onto the left-hand needle.

You may also neaten up the join by working the first two or three stitches of the round with both ends—in other words, the yarn attached to the ball and the tail that remains from casting on. After you have joined and worked several stitches, drop the tail end and continue knitting with the yarn attached to the ball.

The join marks the beginning of your round and can be an invisible "seam line", or a visible one if you choose to make a "seam" stitch. This line will run down the back of your sock leg, and you'll use it later to position other parts of the sock. It is important to note this place.

The classic sock leg is usually worked in a ribbing stitch. Most common are k1,p1 and k2,p2. If you choose a k2,p2 rib, be sure the total number of stitches on your needles is divisible by 4. A variation on this style is to knit several inches of ribbing as a cuff and the rest of the leg to the heel in Stockinette stitch (knit every round). Ribbing at the top of a sock leg allows the fabric to stretch. Because the cuff of the sock generally reaches to the calf, which is wider than the ankle below it, the stretch of the ribbing makes a better fit and helps to keep the sock from drooping.

When the leg is the desired length from the cast-on edge to the beginning of the heel, it's time to work the heel flap. The heel flap is the knitted square that covers the back of the heel. This is the only part of the classic sock that is worked flat, back and forth, rather than in the round.

It is often desirable to reinforce the heel flap, especially if knitting socks that will receive a lot of wear such as skiing or hiking socks, to prolong the life of the heel. Many modern yarns made especially for knitting socks have some nylon content, which makes them stronger. Some skeins are accompanied by a small amount of reinforcing yarn. This reinforcing yarn is usually thinner than the yarn used to knit the sock. You may also reinforce heels with wooly nylon (a thread used with sergers and available at fabric stores), polyester sewing thread, or fine fingering yarn in an appropriate color. In any case, if desired, add the reinforcing yarn when you begin the heel flap. Another way to reinforce a heel when it is worked in Stockinette stitch is to use two ends of your working yarn, alternating ends of yarn stitch by stitch. Alternate the working yarn so that the yarn not being worked is carried across the back of the stitch being worked. This makes the heel flap doubly thick and very strong. This technique also can be used in two-color patterns. Work one stitch with one color and the next stitch with the other. You can either alternate them on every row for a checkerboard pattern or keep the colors on top of each other for stripes.

You can also reinforce the heel of a sock by weaving a strand of the same yarn with which you worked the heel into the heel after the sock is complete. Turn the sock inside out and, using a blunt-point wool needle, weave the yarn back and forth over the inner surface of the heel flap.

The heel flap begins after the last round of the leg has been worked, at the "seam line". At this point, you divide your work in half and only work on the heel stitches. You'll work the other half—the instep stitches—later.

If your socks are one color, divide the stitches this way: starting at the beginning of the round, knit one quarter of the total number of stitches. (For instance, if you have a total of 64 stitches, knit 16 stitches.) Now slip any unworked stitches from the end of the needle you've been working across onto the needle beyond it. Turn the work. This direction is not incorrect—you are now prepared to work back across the stitches you just finished working. Slip the first stitch of this next row as if to purl, then purl until you have the necessary number to equal half of your original stitches on your working needle. If you started with 64 stitches, slip the first stitch, then purl 31 more stitches. These 32 stitches should now all be on one needle. Place all the stitches not worked (there should be 32 of them as well) onto another needle (or two other nee-

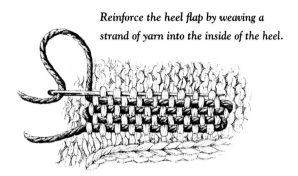

Reinforce the heel flap by weaving a strand of yarn into the inside of the heel.

dles if you prefer). These are the instep stitches, which will wait patiently to be worked until the heel is complete. By beginning the heel in this way, you have added an extra row over one fourth of your stitches (the first 16 you worked). Don't worry, the extra row won't show.

You are now ready to work the heel flap in the pattern called the Heel Stitch. This stitch is found on many historical socks and in countless patterns.

HEEL STITCH

Begin on a right-side row. Slip the first stitch as if to purl, k1 and repeat these two stitches across the row, slipping one and knitting one until you reach the end of the row. The last stitch worked will be a knit stitch. Turn the work and slip the first stitch as if to purl, then purl the rest of the stitches on the wrong-side row. Repeat these two rows for the entire heel flap.

After several rows, you will notice that the right side of your work has a riblike effect, more subtle than regular ribbing. This is due to the ridges created by the slipped stitches, which are running in columns one above the other, every right-side row. These slipped stitches also look bigger than regular knit stitches—and indeed they are, as they stretch over the thread that runs behind them when they are slipped. By recognizing these slipped stitches, you can count your heel-flap rows easily, so you will work exactly the right number. There will be one slipped stitch for every two rows worked.

As the heel flap is worked, and the first stitch of every row is slipped as if to purl, a chained edge is created. This makes one chain-edge stitch for every two rows worked and gives the heel flap smoother edges. Stitches can also be slipped as if to knit at the beginning of every row, which creates a twisted chain stitch. Or you can slip the first stitch of every knit row as if to knit and the first stitch of every purl row as if to purl.

Another way to work the chain-edge stitch for the heel flap is to slip the last stitch of every heel-flap row with the yarn in front (wyf) and knit the first stitch of every heel flap row through the back loop (tbl). Choose the method you like best!

Notes and special considerations:

The heel flap is usually as long as it is wide. As you work, fold the lower left-hand corner of the flap up to the upper right-hand corner to form a triangle. When they meet, the heel flap is long enough. You can also simply work as many rows as there are stitches in the heel flap. (If you have 30 heel-flap stitches, work 30 rows.) Remember that there is one chain-edge stitch for every two rows worked on the heel flap.

If you are making a sock that will have a gusset shaping, you need to create enough rows in the flap to allow you to pick up the necessary stitches along the two sides of the flap to accommodate the flap and the decreases for the gusset shaping. You also need to consider how many stitches will remain after the heel is turned. (See the Common Heel and the Shaped Common Heel in the next chapter.)

If you notice that your hand-knit socks keep creeping down into your shoe, the heel flap may not be deep enough. To correct this annoying problem, simply work a few extra rows of the heel flap. Remember to compensate for these added rows when you pick up your gusset stitches and work the foot of your sock.

Many traditional sock heels were worked in simple Stockinette stitch (which, when working flat, is knit one row, purl one row). Some had garter-stitch edges on the heel flaps, which was achieved by keeping the three to five stitches next to the edge stitch of the heel flap always in knit, while working the rest of the heel-flap stitches in stockinette stitch.

Stockinette stitch is also used for heel flaps decorated with a two-color pattern, such as a geometric design or dancing figures. Heel flaps can also be worked in a contrasting color to the main color of the sock. Historically, for some stockings for everyday wear, the top cuff, rib or welt, the heel, and the toe would be worked in natural-white wool yarn and the rest of the stocking in a dyed or colored wool yarn.

If you want to work the heel flap in a different color than the leg of the sock, you must organize the stitches a little differently than for a single-colored sock. End the leg of the sock at the "seam line". Break the yarn, leaving a 6-in. tail (this will be woven in later). Adjust your stitches so that you have half of the total number of stitches on one needle with the "seam line" centered in the middle of them. These are the heel stitches. Place the other half of the stitches—for the instep—on another needle, or two needles if you prefer. (These instep stitches will be joined in again after the heel is worked.) With the right side of the heel stitches facing you, attach the new color and knit across the row. Turn the work and carry on with the heel flap.

When you've knit the needed number of heel-flap rows, the fun really begins—it's time to turn the heel! You'll work a series of short rows back and forth, centered on the heel flap. The directions below are for a Round Heel. (See Chapter Six for other heel shapings.)

With the right side facing you, knit to the middle of the heel-flap stitches. K2, slip 1 (sl1), k1, pass the slipped stitch over the knit stitch (PSSO), k1. Turn your work. (Ignore the unworked stitches beyond this turning place—they'll be taken care of as you work the heel.) Now sl1, p5, p2 together, p1. Turn your work. *Sl1 as if to purl, knit to within one stitch away from the gap you created when you worked the first decrease, sl1, k1, PSSO, k1. Turn your work. Sl1, purl to within one stitch away from the gap you created when you worked the second decrease, p2 together, p1. Turn your work.* Now repeat these two rows between *s, using up the stitches on each end of the needle until you have none left. On the last two rows, you will have enough stitches to work the decreases, but not the k1 or p1 that follows them. This is correct, so don't worry.

Notice as you shape the heel that after you have worked the first two rows (a right-side row and a wrong-side row), you have the same number of stitches on the ends of the needle on both sides. By counting these stitches after every set of two rows, you can check your work and be sure you haven't missed a stitch. There should always be the same number of stitches waiting at both ends of the needle after you finish the wrong-side row.

Now sit back and look at your work. You have created a Round Heel, the angle that will connect the top "tube" of the leg with the foot, the "tube" you'll make next. In order to create the foot, you'll need to join the stitches of the heel to the instep stitches, which have been left patiently waiting all this time.

Now that the heel is turned, you're ready to begin a right-side row. Knit to the middle of the heel stitches. You are back to the place that corresponds to the spot where you joined the first round. This (visible or invisible) "seam line" running along the back of the sock leg will now mark the beginning of all future rounds. Knit the remaining heel stitches so that all the heel stitches are on one needle.

Now, with the heel needle in your right hand and an empty needle in your left hand, pick up and knit the stitches required for your size along the right side of the heel flap. Look for the whole edge stitch (chain stitch) and either pick up the half of it closest to you or pick up the whole stitch if you prefer. With an empty needle, knit across the instep stitches. With another empty needle, pick up and knit the correct number of stitches along the left side of the heel flap. Onto this same needle, knit the first half of the heel stitches. You should have the second half of the heel stitches and the first group of picked-up stitches on needle #1, the instep stitches on needle #2 and the second group of picked-up stitches and the remaining half of the heel stitches on needle #3. The stitches will stay divided in this way for the rest of the sock.

(If you are using five needles, divide the instep stitches onto two needles. Your back needles will be #1 and #4, and the instep stitches will be on needles #2 and #3.)

Your stitches are again joined into a round, but you have more stitches than you need for the foot, so the extra stitches must be decreased. This step is called shaping the gusset.

On the next round, knit to three stitches away from the end of needle #1, k2 tog, k1. Work across the instep stitches without decreasing. K1 at the beginning of needle #3, sl1 as if to knit, sl1 as if to knit, insert the left-hand needle into the front of the two slipped stitches and knit these two slipped stitches with the right-hand needle (SSK). Then work to the end of the needle.

Work the next round even without decreasing. Repeat these two rounds until you have decreased the number of stitches on each back needle (needles #1 and #3) to equal half the number of stitches on the needle with the instep stitches (#2). (For example, if you have 32 stitches on needle #2, you need to have 16 stitches each on needles #1 and #3.) (Or #1 and #4 if using a set of five needles.)

At this point you can relax and knit around and around until the foot of your sock measures about 2 inches less than the total desired length of the foot, measuring from the back of the heel to the tip of the toe.

Notes and special considerations:

The gussets are worked from stitches picked up along the two sides of the heel flap, after the heel has been turned. These stitches need to be picked up with right sides facing you. To pick up the stitches to join the heel with the instep, first work along the right side of the heel flap to pick up the needed stitches. Then work across the instep stitches and along the left side of the heel flap. (Right and left refer to the sides of the heel flap when the sock is right-side up, as though it is on your foot.)

If the stitches are picked up by knitting through the back loop, they will be tighter and less likely to develop unsightly holes down the sides of the heel. You can work this way when you have made the chain stitches by slipping the first stitch of every heel flap row or when you have slipped the last stitch of every row with the yarn in front and knitted the first stitch of every row through the back loop.

Another traditional way of collecting the gusset stitches is to pick them up without knitting them, and then to begin working the round, knitting into the back of each picked-up loop. This will create the same effect as picking up and knitting through the back loop on one round.

Here is a technique that calls for adding an extra stitch at the beginning and end of the instep needle and decreasing it on the next round. This will help close up the holes that frequently occur at the junction of the back needles to the front one (or ones, if you're using 5 needles). When picking up stitches on each side of the heel flap, you may pick up one extra stitch between the last stitch picked up on the heel flap and the beginning of the instep stitches. Place this extra stitch on the instep needle and work across the instep. Before picking up the stitches on the other side of the heel flap, pick up one extra stitch and place it at the end of the instep needle. On the next round, SSK the first two stitches on the instep needle together and k2 tog the last two stitches on the instep

Half of stitch picked up

Whole stitch picked up

Picking up stitches by knitting through the back loop.

needle to reduce the stitches on the instep needle back to the necessary number.

The gussets can be decreased in a number of similar, yet varied ways. You can begin the decreases on the round directly after the picked-up round and work one round even between each decrease round. It is also possible to work one or two rounds even before beginning the decreases and then to continue the decreases every other round, placing an even round between the decrease rounds. You can also work two even rounds between decrease rounds.

The gusset decreases can be worked on the last three stitches of needle #1 and the first three stitches of needle #3 as in the Classic Sock (p. 59), or they can be worked on the last two and first two stitches of the respective needles, to place them closer to the instep needle.

If you find you need to create a sock for a person with a normal or narrow ankle and a wide foot, don't decrease the gussets down to the same stitch count as at the ankle—leave two or four extra stitches on the heel needles to add the width of the overall foot. When you shape the toe, you can adjust for these extra stitches.

The gussets will have a prettier line if the decreases used mirror each other (see Common Decreases, pp. 50–51). Use a right-leaning decrease when you are ending a needle, as when you decrease at the end of needle #1 by knitting 2 tog. Use a left-leaning decrease when you are beginning a needle, as when you SSK at the beginning of needle #3.

Shaping the Toe

The next step is to shape the toe. All you need to know is what you learned shaping the gussets—they are worked in a similar manner. This toe shaping is a Wedge Toe.

On the next round, knit to three stitches away from the end of needle #1, k2 tog, k1. K1, SSK at the beginning of needle #2, work to three stitches away from the end of this needle, k2 tog, k1. K1 at the beginning of needle #3, SSK, then work to the end of the needle.

Work the next round even without decreasing. Repeat these two rounds until you have decreased the number of stitches by half. Then work the decrease round only until you have 8 stitches remaining. Break off your yarn and thread the end through the remaining stitches. Pull it up tightly and weave the end in. Alternately, you can use the Kitchener stitch to graft the stitches on the top of the toes (needle #2) to the stitches on the bottom of the toes (needles #1 and #3). Weave in the end at the cast-on edge, and get busy making another mate for this little miracle, your first sock!

KITCHENER STITCH

1. Bring the yarn needle through the front st as if to purl, leaving the st on the needle.
2. Bring the yarn needle through the back st as if to knit, leaving the st on the needle.
3. Bring the yarn needle through the same front st as if to knit, and then slip

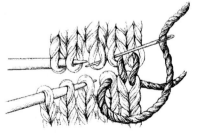

this st off the needle. Bring the yarn needle through the next front st as if to purl, again leaving the st on the needle.
4. Bring the yarn needle through the first back st as if to purl, slip that st off, and then bring the yarn needle through the next back st as if to knit, leaving it on the needle. Repeat steps 3 and 4 until all sts are used up.

A CLASSIC SOCK PATTERN

And some variations on heel and toe

A CLASSIC SOCK

SIZES:

Child [shoe sizes 3 to 7] (Child [shoe sizes 8 to 13], Ladies, Men). Size variations will depend on length of foot.

MATERIALS:

1(1,2,2) skeins of Fingering Weight Sock Yarn (50 grams/approximately 215 yards).

Set of four (or set of five) size #2 8-inch double-point needles, or size to obtain gauge.

Marker

Blunt-Pointed Wool Needle

Gauge: 15 sts and 21 rounds = 2 inches in Stockinette stitch worked in the round.

CAST ON

Cast on loosely 40(48,56,64) sts. Divide these sts evenly onto 3 needles and join into a round, being careful not to twist stitches. This join marks the "seam line" and the beginning of the round.

LEG

Work k1,p1 ribbing or k2,p2 ribbing for 1½ (4,7,9½) inches or desired length to top of heel. Or you may work ribbing as a border or welt to desired length, then switch to Stockinette stitch for desired length of leg to heel.

HEEL FLAP

Add reinforcing yarn if desired. K10(12,14,16) sts. Turn work. Sl1, p19(23,27,31) sts. Place 20(24,28,32) sts remaining onto one needle to be held for instep. Working back and forth on the heel sts only and starting with the right side facing, *sl1, k1, repeat from * across row.

Next row: sl1, purl to end.

Repeat these 2 rows 9(11,13,15) times more. You will have a total of 20(24,28,32) heel rows (10(12,14, 16) chain-edge stitches). End ready to start a right-side row.

TURN THE HEEL

The Round Heel shaping is made with

a series of short rows. Knit to the middle of the row, K2, sl1, k1, PSSO, k1, turn work.

Next row: Sl1, p5, p2 tog, p1, turn.

Next row: Sl1, k to within 1 st away from gap, sl1, k1, PSSO, k1, turn.

Next row: Sl1, p to within 1 st away from gap, p2 tog, p1, turn. Continue in this manner, always working together the 2 sts on each side of the gap.

When all sts have been used up from both sides, knit to the middle of the right-side row. Break off reinforcing thread.

THE HEEL GUSSET

Knit the second half of the heel sts onto the needle containing the first half of the heel stitches. With the same needle, pick up and k10(12,14,16) sts along the right side of heel. With empty needle, work across instep sts. With the remaining empty needle, pick up and k10(12,14,16) sts along left side of heel, and work across the remaining heel sts. You should have half the number of heel sts plus the right-side gusset sts on needle #1, the instep sts on needle #2, and the left-side gusset sts plus half the heel sts on needle #3. If not, adjust your sts to achieve this. The round now begins at the back of the heel.

SHAPE THE GUSSET

On the next round, work to 3 sts away from the end of needle #1, k2 tog, k1. Work across instep sts. At the beginning of needle #3, k1, SSK, work to end.

Next round: Work plain in St st.

Repeat these 2 rounds, decreasing at the end of needle #1 and the beginning of needle #3 until you have a total of 40(48,56,64) sts. You will have 10(12,14,16)stitches on needle #1, 20(24,28,32) on needle #2, and 10(12,14,16) stitches on needle #3. Continue even in St st until foot measures 1¼(1½,2,2¼) inches less than desired length from heel to toe.

SHAPE THE TOE

These instructions are for a Wedge Toe.

Next round: Add reinforcing thread again here, if desired. Work to 3 sts away from end of needle #1, k2 tog, k1. K1, SSK at beginning of needle #2, work to 3 sts away from end of needle #2, k2 tog, k1. K1, SSK at beginning of needle #3, work to end.

Next round: Work plain in St st. Repeat these 2 rounds until you have 20(24,28,32) sts remaining. Now work decreases every round until 8 sts remain. Cut yarn leaving an 8-inch tail. Thread the yarn through a darning needle, draw the end through the remaining stitches and pull them snug. Weave the ends into the inside of the sock.

Block the finished socks under a damp towel or on sock blockers.

HEEL VARIATIONS

In addition to the Round Heel described in Chapter 5 and used in the Classic Sock pattern here, there are a number of ways to shape a heel. The following two heel shapes were discovered in *Modern Knitting Illustrated*, a British knitting book by Jane Koster and Margaret Murray.

THE COMMON HEEL

This is the simplest heel I have run across. It has no decreases, but the Kitchener stitch is used to finish the heel, so it does require some technical know-how.

With an even number of stitches, work the heel flap to the desired length. Include enough rows to equal the number of stitches on the instep needle plus extra rows to equal the number of stitches you wish to decrease on each side of the gusset for shaping. For example, if you had a total of 64 sts in the sock leg at the ankle, 32 of these are instep stitches. By decreasing 4 sts on each side of the gusset, you could create a nice line to the foot. So, knit the

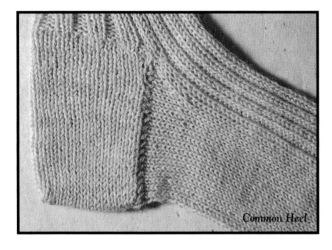

Common Heel

heel flap with 32 rows plus 8 rows for a total of 40 rows. Remember to make a chain-edge stitch at both sides of the heel flap.

When the heel flap is complete, knit to the middle of the row. Break off your yarn, leaving about a 20-inch tail. Hold the two needles containing the heel stitches parallel, with the right sides of the work facing you. With a blunt-point needle, graft the two sets of 16 sts together with the Kitchener stitch.

At the place where you finished the Kitchener stitch, join yarn and pick up and knit 20 sts along the right side of the heel flap to the instep needle. Work across the stitches on the instep needle, and pick up and knit 20 sts along the left side of the heel flap, ending where you began at the bottom of the foot.

Now work the gusset decreases as for the Classic Sock, to achieve a total of 64 sts or 16 heel sts each on needles #1 and #3, and 32 instep stitches on needle #2.

(If using five needles, divide the instep stitches in half so that you have 16 sts on each instep needle.)

You'll notice that the Common Heel has a little nipple of fabric at the back. This will flatten out with wear, but if it bothers you, try the next heel style, which is similar to this one, but won't leave a nipple.

THE SHAPED COMMON HEEL

This heel has a more refined shape than the Common Heel and fits very well.

On an even number of stitches, for example, a sock with 32 stitches for the heel flap, work the heel flap as for the Common Heel for 32 rows, ending ready to begin a RS row. Remember to make a chain-edge stitch at both sides of the heel flap. Now place a marker (M) at the middle of the heel stitches.

Sl1, work to 2 sts before M, k2 tog, slip M, SSK, work to end of row, turn work. Sl1, purl across the row, turn.

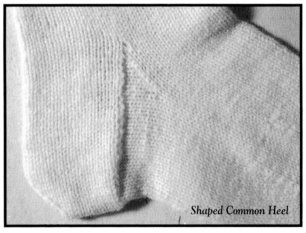

Shaped Common Heel

Repeat these 2 rows 4 times more, for a total of 10 rows. End by stopping at the M in the middle of the row on the last WS row. Remove the M.

Break off your yarn leaving about a 20-inch tail. Hold the two needles that contain the heel stitches parallel, with right sides facing you. With a blunt-point needle, graft the two sets of 11 sts together with the Kitchener stitch.

At the point where you finished the Kitchener stitch, join yarn and pick up and knit 21 sts along the right side of the heel flap to the instep needle. Work across the instep needle and pick up and knit the 21 sts along the left side of the heel flap, ending where you began at the bottom of the foot. Now work the gusset decreases as for the Classic Sock, to achieve a total of 64 sts or 16 sts each on needles #1 and #3 and the 32 instep sts on needle #2.

Perhaps you've worked a purl-stitch "seam" down the center back of the leg and you want to work this heel shaping over an odd number of stitches. Simply decrease to shape the back of the heel on each side of the purl stitch or center stitch on the heel flap. On the last row, work the center stitch together with its neighbor to achieve an even number of stitches so that you can graft them together.

THE BALBRIGGAN HEEL

This is another heel shaping from *Modern Knitting Illustrated*. It shares its name with Balbriggan, Ireland, a village north of Dublin, which also gave its name to a knitted fabric, made from Sea Island cotton, used for underwear and hosiery.

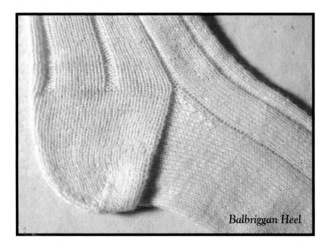

Balbriggan Heel

This heel is worked on a sock with 80 sts in the ankle. The heel, worked over 40 st, looks nice in Stockinette stitch. It can be reinforced by carrying two strands of the same color yarn or by adding in a reinforcing yarn as the heel is knitted (see pp. 53–54). Remember to make a chain-edge stitch at both sides of the heel flap.

To work the heel flap in one color, work to 20 sts beyond the beginning of the round, then turn and begin the heel flap by purling 40 sts and placing a marker at the center of the heel flap. The next WS row is row #1. Work until you have a total of 35 rows, ending ready to begin a RS row.

Row 1: (K8, k2 tog) 2 times, M, (k2 tog, k8) 2 times.
Row 2 and all even rows: Purl.
Row 3: K8, k2 tog, k6, (k2 tog) twice, k6, k2 tog, k8.
Row 5: K8, k2 tog, k4, (k2 tog) twice, k4, k2 tog, k8.
Row 7: K8, k2 tog, k2,(k2 tog) twice, k2, k2 tog, k8.
Row 9: K8, (k2 tog) 4 times, k8.

Work to marker, remove marker, then graft the remaining two sets of 10 sts together with the Kitchener stitch.

The original pattern for the Balbriggan Heel calls for k2 tog decreases. It can also be worked using SSK for the decreases before the marker and k2 tog for the decreases after the marker. By working them this way, the angles of the decreases will mirror each other.

Beginning at the point where the two sides of the heel are joined, join yarn and pick up and knit 23 sts. With an empty needle, knit across the 40 instep sts. With an empty needle, pick up and knit 23 sts, ending at the beginning of the round.

Next round: Work to within 3 sts from end of needle #1, k2 tog, k1. Work across instep sts. K1, SSK at the beginning of needle #3, work to end of round. Work 1 round plain.

Repeat these 2 rounds until you have 16 sts on each of the back needles. These joined with the 40 sts on the instep needle will give you 72 sts. Continue working the foot and toe as desired.

(If working with five needles, divide the instep stitches onto two needles.)

The original pattern for the Balbriggan Heel has the knitter decrease the gusset to 72 sts for the foot from 80 sts at the ankle. This number of foot stitches is not set in stone—you may decrease to any number of sts for the foot that gives you the fit you desire and that works with your pattern. The general rule is to decrease the foot back to

worked. End having completed a WS row.

The gusset shaping is the same as for the other heels discussed. Pick up and knit stitches on the sides of the heel flap to equal half the number of rows you worked in the heel flap. Work the decreases to narrow the foot until you have the same number of stitches that you started with at the ankle.

Half-Handerchief Heel

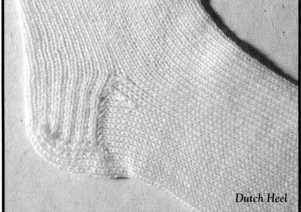

Dutch Heel

the number of stitches you had at the ankle before the start of the heel flap. The Balbriggan pattern, while not following the general rule, works well as it is designed.

THE HALF-HANDKERCHIEF HEEL

This heel, which began in my notes as the V heel, is a variation on the Round Heel but is more narrow and fitted. It's worked over an even number of stitches.

When the heel flap is the desired length, work to the center of the heel sts, SSK, k1, turn work. Sl1, p1, p2 tog, p1, turn. Sl1, work to 1 st before the gap (where the last row turned), SSK, k1, turn. Sl1, p to 1 st before the gap, p2 tog, p1, turn. Continue in this manner until all sts are

THE DUTCH HEEL

This heel shaping, also known as the Square Heel, and the next one, the Band Heel, are very similar. The Dutch Heel has shaped gussets, as do the heels already discussed; the Band Heel does not.

The Dutch Heel is very neat and fitted. It has a band that runs under the heel, and the first decision is how wide to make this band. One traditional way to plan a Dutch Heel is to divide the number of stitches in the heel flap into approximate thirds and then work the band over the center third. (For example, a sock with 56 sts might have a band 8 sts wide.) In some Estonian and Latvian patterns, the knitter divides heel stitches onto three separate needles and then works the heel shaping across them.

Work the heel flap as for the previous heels. When you are ready to turn the heel, place a marker (M) at the center of the sts. With RS facing you, knit to 3 sts beyond M, SSK, turn. Sl1, P6 (you will be 3 sts beyond M on the WS), p2 tog, turn. Sl1, K6, SSK, turn. Sl1, P6, p2 tog, turn. Repeat last 2 rows until all sts have been worked, ending having completed a WS row.

You can adjust the width of the band under the heel by working fewer or more stitches beyond the center stitch when you begin the shaping, keeping this number constant as you turn the heel.

The Dutch Heel can also be worked by continuing the reinforcing Heel Stitch (see page 54) from the heel flap right through the heel turning. This will create a slightly padded, reinforced heel that will be less likely to wear out.

THE BAND HEEL

The Band Heel looks very similar to the Dutch Heel, but has no gusset shaping. The shaping actually occurs while making the heel flap. I discovered this style of heel turning in *Bondestrick,* a Danish book about traditional stockings.

Band Heel

Begin with 80 sts at the ankle. Work 24 rows for the heel flap over 40 sts, ending ready to begin a RS row. You will have 12 chain-edge stitches at each edge of the heel flap. Work the edge-stitch in whatever way you choose (see p. 55).

Row 1: Edge-stitch, k14, k2 tog, k6, SSK, k14, edge-stitch.

Row 2, 4, 6 and 8: Edge-stitch, p to last stitch, edge-stitch.

Row 3: Same as the first row, but work 13 sts instead of 14 sts after the first edge st and before the last edge st.

Row 5: Same as the first row, but work 12 sts instead of 14 sts after the first edge st and before the last edge st.

Row 7: Same as the first row, but work 11 sts instead of 14 sts after the first edge st and before the last edge st.

Upon completing these 8 rows, there should be 32 sts remaining on the heel flap.

Now turn the heel as follows:

Row 1 (RS): Edge-stitch, k18, SSK, turn work.

Row 2: Sl1, p6, p2 tog, turn.

Row 3: Sl1, k6, SSK, turn.

Row 4: Sl1, p6, p2 tog, turn.

Repeat rows 3 and 4 until all heel sts are worked.

There will be 8 sts remaining. Divide these 8 sts in half, and place them on two needles; they will become the first 4 sts on needle #1 and the last 4 sts on needle #3. Pick up and knit 16 sts on each side of the heel flap, working across the instep stitches to join the foot into a round. Continue working the foot with no decreases to the length needed.

THE PEASANT HEEL

The Peasant Heel is unique. It has no heel flap, and the heel is worked as the last part of the sock, rather than midway through the process. This type of heel is found on stockings and socks from the Middle East, the Ukraine, and the Balkans. You'll need a set of five needles to work this heel (four to carry the stitches and one to use as the working needle).

Cast on 60 sts and work the sock leg. When the leg is the desired length to the center of the heel, you need to prepare for the addition of the heel, which will be done after the rest of the sock is finished.

To do this, knit the back half of the leg stitches (those that will form the heel) with a piece of waste yarn. To center the heel on the back seam of the leg, work as follows: work 45 sts of the next round in the main color. Then, work the last 15 sts of the round and the first 15 sts of the following round with the waste yarn. Break off the waste yarn. Now adjust the 30 sts you just worked onto 2 needles so that you can continue from the place you left off the working yarn and complete the round using the main color.

For a lady's sock with a medium-length leg, work about 7½ inches of leg length before you add in the waste yarn for the heel. The toe shaping will begin approximately 4 inches after the waste yarn is added. You'll have to adjust these figures for different sizes of feet or for longer or shorter sock lengths.

Now, continue knitting in your chosen pattern. When the sock is complete up to the toe, it's time to finish the heel. Carefully pull out the waste yarn. The result will be 30 sts on one side and 29 sts on the other. Place these stitches onto 4 needles, beginning at one side of the heel opening—15 sts on each of three needles and 14 sts on the 4th needle. Beginning at the edge that precedes the two needles that are each holding 15 sts, and using your working yarn, pick up and knit through the back loop (k tbl) 1 new st, then knit across the next 15 sts. With an empty needle, knit across the next 15 stitches. With an empty needle, pick up and k tbl a new st, then knit across the next 15 sts. With an empty needle, knit across the next 14 sts and pick up and k tbl one new st. You should

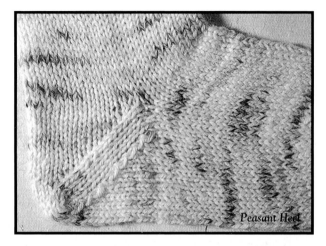

Peasant Heel

have 16 sts on needle #1, 15 sts on needle #2, 16 sts on needle #3 and 15 st on needle #4, for a total of 62 sts.

Next you'll shape the heel. You can begin to shape it right away or, if you want to give the heel some additional length, you can first work several rounds even. The heel is shaped very much like the Wedge Toe (p. 60), by decreasing at both sides of the heel evenly to bring it to a rounded point.

Begin the shaping at the side edge, where the round begins, as follows: *K1, SSK, k13, k12, k2 tog, k1, repeat from * across the next two needles.

Depending on the desired depth of the heel and the number of rounds you worked before beginning to decrease, you can work the decrease round every round or every other round until you have approximately the number of stitches to equal 1/2 inch of gauge remaining on each of the 4 needles. (For example, if your gauge is 8 stitches per inch, work decreases until you have 4 stitches on each needle.) Place the stitches on needles #1 and #2 together onto one needle and do the same for the stitches on needles #3 and #4. Graft the two sets of stitches together with the Kitchener stitch.

TOE VARIATIONS

As you near the end of your sock, there are a few plans that must be made. Determine how many rows your toe shaping will require. This figure, divided by your row gauge, will tell you the length of knitting your toe shaping will be. The foot must be worked to the desired total finished length minus the length needed for the toe shaping.

The most common way to work a toe is to decrease at both sides of the sock evenly. This brings the toe to a gradual rounded point. The first six styles of toe decreasing presented here are worked in this way. The differences between them are their completed lengths or widths, and the number of stitches worked between the decreases.

The following instructions require a set of four needles—three to hold the stitches and one as a working needle. The stitches are divided with half of them on needle #2 and one quarter each on needles #1 and #3. The division between needles #1 and #3 is centered at the back of the heel or under the foot, in line with the tail that remained when you cast on—the "seam line". You will decrease at the end of needle #1, at the beginning of needle #2, at the end of needle #2, and at the beginning of needle #3.

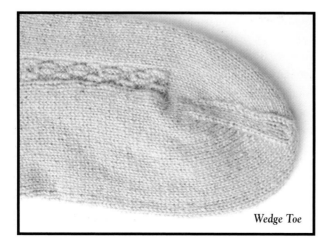

Wedge Toe

If you prefer to use five needles, simply divide the instep stitches (those stitches on needle #2) onto two needles. In this case, you will be decreasing at the end of needle #1, at the beginning of needle #2, at the end of needle #3, and at the beginning of needle #4.

To finish off any of these toes, you can cut yarn leaving an eight-inch tail, thread the yarn through a darning needle, draw the end through the remaining stitches and pull them snug, and then weave the ends into the inside of sock. Or you can graft the two sets of stitches together with the Kitchener stitch.

THE WEDGE TOE

When the foot measures the desired length less the toe shaping, work as follows beginning at the "seam line".

Round 1: Work to 3 sts from end of needle #1, k2 tog, k1. K1, SSK at the beginning of needle #2, knit to 3 sts away from the end of needle #2, k2 tog, k1. K1, SSK at the beginning of needle #3, knit to end of round.

Round 2: Work plain.

Repeat these two rounds until you have reduced the number of sts by half on each needle. Now continue to work the decrease round only until you have approximately the number of stitches to equal 1 inch of gauge on the instep needle and the same amount on the two back needles combined. Knit the remaining sts on needle #1 onto needle #3 and graft the two sets of sts together with the Kitchener stitch, or draw the stitches together as for the Classic Sock.

THE WEDGE TOE VARIATION #1

This is a longer toe shaping. When the foot measures the desired length less the toe shaping, work as follows beginning at the "seam line".

Round 1: Work to 3 sts from end of needle #1, k2 tog, k1. K1, SSK at the beginning of needle #2, knit to 3 sts

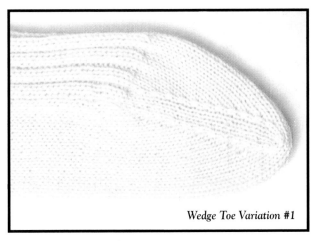

Wedge Toe Variation #1

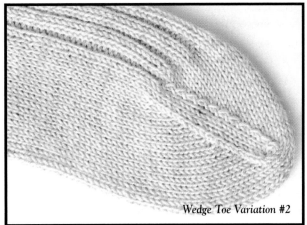

Wedge Toe Variation #2

away from end of needle #2, k2 tog, k1. K1, SSK at beginning of needle #3, work to end of round.

Round 2 and 3: Work plain.

Repeat these 3 rounds until you have approximately the number of stitches to equal 1 inch of gauge remaining on the instep needle and the same amount on the back needles combined. Knit the remaining sts on needle #1 onto needle #3 and graft the two sets of sts together with the Kitchener stitch, or draw the stitches together as for the Classic Sock.

THE WEDGE TOE VARIATION #2

This is a mid-length version of the two previous toe shapings. When the foot measures the desired length less the toe shaping, work as follows beginning at the "seam line".

Round 1: Work to 3 sts from end of needle #1, k2 tog, k1. K1, SSK at the beginning of needle #2, work to 3 sts away from end of needle #2, k2 tog, k1. K1, SSK at beginning of needle #3, work to end of round.

Round 2: Work plain.

Repeat these two rounds until you have approximately the number of stitches to equal 1 inch of gauge re-

maining on the instep needle and the same amount on the back needles combined. Knit the remaining sts on needle #1 onto needle #3 and graft the two sets of sts together with the Kitchener stitch, or draw the stitches together as for the Classic Sock.

WIDE TOE, VERSION #1

When the foot measures the desired length less the toe shaping, work as follows beginning at the "seam line".

Round 1: Work to 4 sts away from end of needle #1, k2

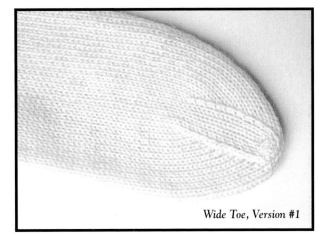

Wide Toe, Version #1

tog, k2. K2, SSK at the beginning of needle #2, work to 4 sts away from the end of needle #2, k2 tog, k2. K2, SSK at the beginning of needle #3 and work to end of round.

Round 2: Work plain.

Repeat these 2 rounds until you have half of your original stitches. Then decrease every round until you have approximately the number of stitches to equal 1 inch of gauge remaining on the instep needle and the same amount on the back needles combined. Knit the remaining sts on needle #1 onto needle #3 and graft the two sets of sts together with the Kitchener stitch, or draw the stitches together as for the Classic Sock.

WIDE TOE, VERSION #2

When the foot measures the desired length less the toe shaping, work as follows beginning at the "seam line".

Round 1: Work to 6 sts away from end of needle #1, k2 tog, k4. K4, SSK at beginning of needle #2. Work to 6 sts away from end of needle, k2 tog, k4. K4, SSK at the beginning of needle #3 and work to end of round.

Rounds 2, 3, 4: Work even with no decreases.

Round 5: Work same as Round 1.

Rounds 6, 7: Work even with no decreases.

Round 8: Work same as Round 1.

Round 9: Work even with no decreases.

Round 10: Work same as Round 1.

Repeat these last two rounds until you have approximately the number of stitches to equal 1 to 1½ inches of gauge remaining on needle #2 and the same amount on needles #1 and #3 combined. Knit the sts on needle #1 onto needle #3 and graft the two sets of sts together with the Kitchener stitch, or draw the stitches together as for the Classic Sock.

DOUBLE-DECREASE TOE

This toe works well if you are working with a number of stitches, that when divided, yields two uneven numbers. For example, 50 divided by 2 equals 25. If you have 25 stitches total on your back needles (needles #1 and #3) and 25 stitches on your instep needle, this toe shaping will work nicely. The theory behind this style of shaping is similar to the previous ones; however, each set of decreases are worked at the same time, so you work decreases only twice in a round, instead of four times.

When the foot measures the desired length less the toe shaping, work as follows:

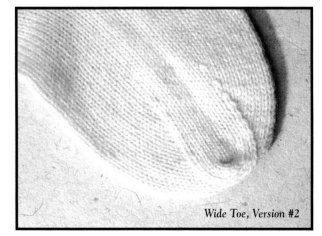

Wide Toe, Version #2

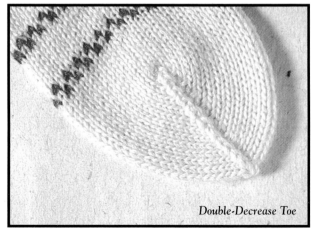

Double-Decrease Toe

Round 1: Beginning at the "seam line", work to 2 sts away from the end of needle #1. *Slip 2 stitches at the same time as if to knit, k1 from needle #2 onto needle #1 and pass the 2 slipped stitches over the knitted stitch*. With an empty needle, work across needle #2 to the last 2 sts and repeat between *s. Complete the round.

Round 2: Work even without decreasing.

Repeat these two rounds until you have decreased approximately half of the sts. Now work the decrease round only until approximately one eighth of the original sts remain. Break the yarn and pull it through the remaining sts. Tighten the yarn and weave it in.

Round Toe

ROUND TOE

Toes can also have a rounded shape. They are formed by working the decreases evenly spaced all around the toe, rather than just at the sides.

This toe is worked over a number of stitches divisible by 8. The round begins at the center of the heel.

Dec Round 1: *K6, K2 tog, repeat from * all around. Work 6 rounds plain.

Dec Round 2: *K5, K2 tog, repeat from * all around. Work 5 rounds plain.

Dec Round 3: *K4, K2 tog, repeat from * all around. Work 4 rounds plain.

Continue in this manner working one less stitch between each decrease and one fewer plain round until you work only one plain round. K2 tog all around. Thread the end of the yarn onto a blunt-point needle and pass the yarn through all remaining sts and pull them tight.

STAR TOE

This toe shaping is worked with the stitches divided evenly onto four needles with a fifth needle as a working needle. The round begins at the "seam line".

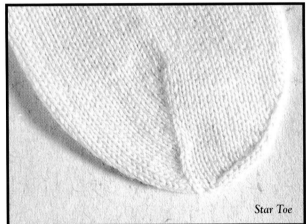

Star Toe

Round 1: Knit tog the last 2 sts on every needle.

Round 2: Work even without decreasing.

Work these two rounds 6 times, then work Round 1 until there are 8 sts remaining. Thread the end of the yarn onto a blunt-point needle and pass the yarn through all remaining sts and pull them tight.

This toe can be lengthened by adding more plain rounds between the decrease rounds or shortened by working the decreases on every round.

SEVEN

THE PATTERNS

Socks for all the world's feet

The designs in the following chapter were all inspired by traditional, historic

references. In some cases a sock or stocking in a museum collection was studied and then

the design created as a reproduction. In others, after reading descriptions or looking at

photographs or drawings, I let my imagination guide me to a workable design. Each sock

or stocking is designed to be useful and wearable for our times and each design contains

techniques found in the previous chapters. If you knit all of the designs offered here, you

will have worked through all of the techniques as well as all of the heel and toe shap-

ings described in this book.

STOCKINGS WITH CLOCKS

This pair of knee-length stockings was inspired by the country stockings found in many parts of Europe. The clocks, a name probably derived from the resemblance of the ankle design to the hands of a clock, have been created with knit and purl stitches. The silk stockings of the wealthy often had embroidery or fancy patterns at the ankles and the style was adopted for general use.

On these stockings, there is a fancy pattern down the back of the leg to decorate the "seam line" and to aid in working the leg shaping. These stockings have a Round Heel and a four-sectioned Star Toe. The pattern fits a man's leg as it is written. Using one needle size smaller will tighten up the gauge and make smaller stockings suitable for a woman's leg.

Materials: Brown Sheep Company's Nature Spun 3-ply sport (100% wool, 100g/approx. 368 yards) #730 Natural, 2 skeins.

Set of five #1 double-point needles or size to give gauge.

Gauge: 15 sts and 22 rounds = 2 inches over Stockinette stitch worked in the round.

LEG

CO 88 sts using the Continental method. Divide the sts as follows: 27 sts on needle #1, 34 sts on needle #2, and 27 sts on needle #3. (Knit with needle #4—needle #5 will be used for the toe.) Join into a round being careful not to twist sts. This join marks the "seam line" and beginning of the round.

Round 1: Knit.

Round 2: Purl.

Border Pattern (see graph)

Round 1: *K1, p1, k2; repeat from *.

Round 2: *P1, k3; repeat from *.

Repeat these 2 rounds for 2 inches. End with Round 2.

Seam pattern (see graph)

Round 1: [K1, p1] twice, knit to last 2 sts, p1, k1. Continue in established pattern with 2 seed sts running down the center back of the stocking. Work until stocking measures 4½ inches.

SHAPE CALF

*Seed 2, k1, p1, SSK, work to last 4 sts of round, k2 tog, p1, k1. Work 5 rounds even.

Repeat from * 9 more times for a total of 10 repeats (20 sts decreased). AT THE SAME TIME, on the 6th decrease round, begin Clock Pattern. Work according to graph centering the first st of clock pattern (a purl stitch) on the 22nd st and the 57th st of the round. Work to end of round. 68 sts remain.

Continue even in established pattern until the leg measures 15 inches total or desired length to top of heel flap.

Adjust the sts so that there are 17 sts on needle #1, 34 sts on needle #2, and 17 sts on needle #3, and so that the "seam line" is between needles #1 and #3.

DIVIDE FOR HEEL

Work in pattern as established across the first 16 sts on needle #1 with needle #3, sl1 wyf. The seed sts will be in the center of the needle. There are 34 sts on the heel needle and 34 sts on needle #2 to be held for instep. Discontinue Seam Pattern but continue Clock Pattern. Turn the work.

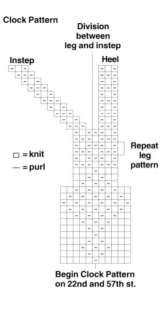

Clock Pattern

Division between leg and instep

Instep

Heel

☐ = knit

— = purl

Repeat leg pattern

Begin Clock Pattern on 22nd and 57th st.

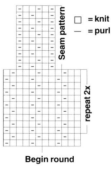

Border and Seam Pattern

Seam pattern

☐ = knit

— = purl

repeat 2x

Begin round

Row 1: K1 tbl, work 3 sts as established, p26 sts, work 3 sts as established, sl1 wyf. Turn.

Row 2: K1 tbl, work 32 sts as established, sl1 wyf. Turn.

Keeping Clock Pattern running down the edges of the heel flap, repeat these last two rows 16 more times for a total of 17 repeats. End with Row 1 ready to begin a RS row (34 rows total).

TURN HEEL

K19, k2 tog tbl, k1, turn. Sl1, p5, p2 tog, p1, turn.

*Sl1, knit to within one stitch of the gap, K2 tog tbl, k1, turn. Sl1, purl to within one stitch of the gap, p2 tog, p1, turn.

Repeat from * until all sts of flap have been worked. End ready to begin a RS row. There are 20 heel sts.

GUSSETS

Knit across 20 heel sts, pick up and k17 sts tbl along the right side of the heel flap. With an empty needle, work across the instep sts in pattern following the instep graph. With an empty needle pick up and k17 sts tbl along the left side of the heel flap; then knit the first 10 sts from the heel needle onto this last needle. There are 27 sts on needle #1, 34 instep sts on needle #2, and 27 sts on needle #3.

SHAPE GUSSETS

Round 1: Knit to 2 sts away from the end of needle #1; k2 tog tbl. Work in established pattern across needle #2. K2 tog at the beginning of needle #3. Knit to end of round.

Round 2: Work even in established pattern.

Repeat these last 2 rounds 9 more times for a total of 10 repeats. There are 17 sts on needles #1 and #3, and 34 instep sts on needle #2. Work even in established patterns on these 68 sts for 1 1/2 inches more. Discontinue Clock Pattern. Change to Stockinette stitch. Work even until length of foot measures approximately 2 1/2 inches less than desired length from heel to toe.

SHAPE TOE

Divide the 34 instep sts onto 2 needles.

Round 1: K2 tog at the end of each needle.

Round 2: Work even in established pattern.

Repeat these last two rounds until there are 9 sts on each of four needles.

Now work Round 1 (the decrease round) only until there are 2 sts on each needle.

Break off the yarn leaving a 10-inch tail. Thread a blunt-point needle; draw it through the remaining sts. Tighten up to finish the toe.

Weave in ends. Block socks under a damp towel or on sock blockers.

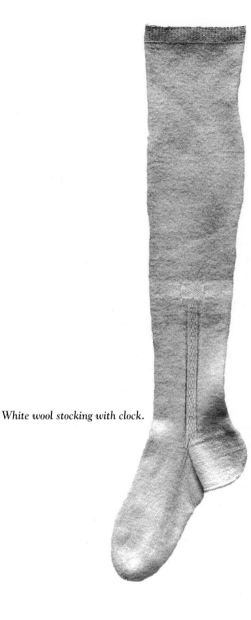

White wool stocking with clock.

The unique shaping for these stockings came from a Husfliden pattern from the 1950's. It intrigued me because I had never seen it done before and it seemed so logical. Rather than decreasing down the back of the leg at the seam line, the decreases are done on one single round just below the widest part of the calf line. It requires working the leg pattern in stripes that allow the decreases to fit in and not disturb the design. The heel flap is worked in two-color pattern knitting, which decorates and reinforces, and a Dutch Heel is used for the heel shaping. The entire foot is patterned, with a "salt and pepper" design continuing through to the end of the Wedge Toe shaping. These stockings will fit a man or a woman.

Materials: Dale of Norway's Heilo (100% wool, 50g/109 yards)
#0090 Black, 4 skeins; #0004 Light Grey, 3 skeins; #4018 Red,
1 skein.

Set of four #3 double-point needles or size to give gauge.

Gauge: 14 sts and 15 rounds = 2 inches over pattern worked in the
round.

LEG

CO 84 sts with Black using the Continental method. Divide the
sts evenly onto 3 needles. Join into a round being careful not to twist
sts. This join marks the "seam line" and beginning of the round.

Rounds 1–3: *K2, p2; repeat from *. Join Light Grey.

Round 4: Knit with Light Grey.

Round 5: With Light Grey, *k2, p2; repeat from *.

Round 6: Knit with Black.

Rounds 7 & 8: With Black, *k2, p2; repeat from *.

Rounds 9–11: Repeat Rounds 4-6. Break off Light Grey.

Rounds 12–14: *K2, p2 repeat from *. Attach Red.

Work graph A as shown. Break off Red. Join Light Grey. Work
graph B until stocking measures 9 inches total. End having just finished round 4 of graph B.

CALF SHAPING

Round 5: Work in established pattern for 10 sts, *sl2 sts at the
same time as if to knit, k1, p2sso, work 9 sts in established pattern.
Repeat from * 5 times more, then work 9 sts in established pattern,
sl2 sts at the same time as if to knit, k1 (this is the first st of needle
#1), p2sso. The round now begins with Light Grey as shown in
Graph B After Decreases. 70 sts remain.

Continue even in established patterns until stocking measures
15 inches total or desired length to top of heel flap. Break yarns.

DIVIDE FOR HEEL

Place the first 19 sts and the last 20 sts of the round together
onto one needle. These 39 sts are the heel sts. Place the remaining
31 sts onto another needle to be held for the instep.

This next row sets up the heel flap pattern.

With right side facing, join yarns, sl1, *k2 Black, k2 tog Black,
k3 Light Grey, k3 Black, k3 Light Grey, k2 tog Black, k2 Black* k3
Light Grey. Repeat between *'s once ending k1 Light Grey.

Continue according to graph C. Slip the first st of every row
and work the last st of every row with Light Grey. Repeat graph C
a total of 4 times. End with Row 6 ready to begin a RS row (24 rows

Graph A

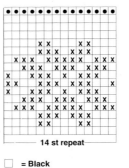

14 st repeat

Graph B

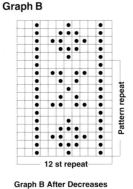

Pattern repeat

12 st repeat

 = Black

 = Red

 = Light Grey

Graph C

Graph B After Decreases

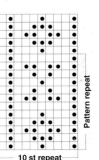

Pattern repeat

10 st repeat

total). Break off yarns. Reinforcing yarn may be added here to
strengthen the bottom of the heel or work using two strands of
Black, alternating them across the heel turn.

TURN HEEL

With an empty needle, slip 11 sts as to purl. Attach Black. K12,
SSK, turn.

*Sl1, p11, p2 tog, turn. Sl1, k11, SSK, turn. Repeat from * until
all sts are worked. End ready to begin a RS row. There are 13 heel
sts.

GUSSETS

K6 sts with Black, attach Light Grey, [k1 Light Grey, k1 Black]
3 times, k1 Light Grey. Pick up and k14 sts tbl along right side of
the heel flap. With an empty needle, work across 31 instep sts in
established pattern. With an empty needle, pick up and k14 sts tbl
along the left side of the heel flap beginning with Light Grey and
alternating Black and Light Grey; then knit the first 6 sts from the
heel needle onto this last needle. There are 21 sts on needle #1, 31
instep sts on needle #2, and 20 sts on needle #3, and the "seam line"

is between needles #1 and #3.

As you work the foot, the pattern of Black and Light Grey sts alternates every row. If you have a Black st on one row, work it Light Grey on the next row.

Round 1: Work in alternating Black and Light Grey pattern to 2 sts from the end of needle #1, k2 tog with Light Grey. Work across instep sts in established pattern. SSK with Light Grey at the beginning of needle #3. Work to end of round in established pattern.

Round 2: Work even in established pattern.

Always keep the last st on needle #1 and the first st on needle #3 in Light Grey.

Repeat these last 2 rounds until you have 16 sts on needle #1, 31 sts on needle #2, and 15 sts on needle #3. Work even in established pattern until foot length measures 3 inches less than desired finished length ending with row 5 or 11 of graph B on instep sts.

SHAPE TOE

Round 1: Knit to 2 sts away from the end of needle #1; k2 tog with Light Grey. K1 with Black at beginning of needle #2; then SSK the next 2 sts together with Light Grey. Work alternating k1 Black, k1 Light Grey across needle #2 to last 3 sts; k2 tog with Light Grey, k1 Black. SSK first 2 sts on needle #3 with Light Grey. Knit to end of round.

Round 2: Work one round even in established patterns.

Repeat these last 2 rounds until you have 11 sts on needle #1, 21 sts on needle #2, and 10 sts on needle #3. On the next decrease round, work even in patt without decreases on needles #1 and #3, and work 2 decreases on needle #2 same as before. When this round is finished there are 11 sts on needle #1, 19 sts on needle #2, and 10 sts on needle #3. Now work Round 1 (decrease round) on every round until you have 5 sts on needle #1, 7 sts on needle #2, and 4 sts on needle #3. Work across the sts on needle #1 in pattern with needle #3, and knit the last 2 sts tog with Light Grey. Break yarn leaving a 10-inch tail. Thread a blunt-point needle. Draw it through the remaining sts. Tighten up to finish the toe.

Weave in ends. Block socks under a damp towel or on sock blockers.

MAMLUKE SOCKS

*T*he inspiration for these decorative socks comes from the collection of the Textile Museum in Washington, D.C. The socks are very typical of Islamic footwear of its period, which is the fifteenth to sixteenth centuries. The band of repeated Cufic style Arabic letters above the heel and before the toe shaping spells "Allah". The heel shaping is similar to a Round Heel, however it is made with a series of short rows in their most simple form. The toe is starlike. It decreases in eight sets of two blue stitches. These are then paired and a natural-colored knit stitch is placed between the pairs. These socks are sized for a woman.

Materials: Berroco's Wendy Guernsey 5-ply (100% wool, 100g/approx. 245 yards) #674 Smoke Blue, 1 skein; #500 Natural, 1 skein.

Set of five #2 double-point needles or size to give gauge.

Gauge: 16 sts and 16 rounds = 2 inches over pattern worked in the round.

LEG

CO 70 sts with Smoke Blue, using the English method. Divide the sts evenly onto 4 needles. Join into a round being careful not to twist sts. This join marks the "seam line" and beginning of the round.

K1, P1 Ribbing

Round 1: *K1, p1. Repeat from * to end of round.

Work Round 1 for 3 rounds total.

Begin leg pattern according to graph A. On last round of graph A (Smoke Blue round), inc 1 st in first st and 1 st in last st. 72 sts total. Adjust sts on needle so you have 18 on each needle and the "seam line" is between needles #1 and #4. Work graph B to completion.

DIVIDE FOR HEEL

The heel is worked on needles #1 and #4. It is created by working a series of short rows without any decreases. There are 18 sts each on heel needles #1 and #4, and 18 sts each on needles #2 and #3 to be held for instep. Begin at "seam line" and work the heel as follows:

Row 1: [K1 Natural, k1 Smoke Blue] 2 times. Turn.

Row 2: Sl1, [p1 Natural, p1 Smoke Blue] 3 times, p1 Natural. Turn.

Row 3: Sl1, [k1 Smoke Blue, k1 Natural] 4 times, k1 Smoke Blue. Turn.

Row 4: Sl1, [p1 Natural, p1 Smoke Blue] 5 times, p1 Natural. Turn.

Repeat these last two rows, slipping the first st of every row, alternating the established colors, and working two sts beyond the last two sts worked on the preceding row of the same side. On the last round, knit to the center of the heel (in line with the "seam line") with RS facing. There will be 18 sts on each needle.

Continue working circularly following graph C. Work until foot measures $5\frac{1}{4}$ inches from back of heel or $3\frac{1}{2}$ inches less than desired finished length. Adjust length of foot by working one more or one less diamond pattern repeat in graph C.

Graph A

Inc 2 sts evenly

☐ = Smoke Blue
✕ = Natural

10 st repeat

Graph B

8 st repeat

6 st repeat

8 st repeat

Graph C

6 st repeat

Graph D

Dec 8 sts evenly

8 st repeat

Graph E

16 st repeat

☐ = Smoke Blue
✕ = Natural
■ = Dec st

Work graph D. On last round of graph D (Natural round), dec 8 sts (k2 tog) evenly spaced. 64 sts total; 16 sts on each needle.

SHAPE TOE

Work first 6 rounds of graph E.

Round 7: [K1 Natural, SSK using Smoke Blue, follow graph to last 2 sts on needle, k2 tog using Smoke Blue] 4 times. Continue according to graph E, decreasing every other round by k1, SSK at the beginning of a needle and k2 tog at the end until 4 sts remain on each needle. Note that the last two decrease rounds do not have a plain round between them.

Next round: [K1 Natural, sl 2 sts at the same time as if to knit, k1 with Smoke Blue, p2sso] 4 times. 2 sts remain on each needle.

Next round: [K2 tog with Natural] 4 times. There are 4 sts total. Break yarn leaving a 10-inch tail. Thread a blunt-point needle. Draw it through the remaining sts. Tighten up to finish the toe.

Weave in ends. Block socks under a damp towel or on sock blockers.

Islamic Stockings

This colorful pair of socks was inspired by a similar pair in the Royal Ontario Museum in Toronto, Canada. These stockings were bordered at the top by a band of lace. The long legs were of natural white wool and only the heel and the toe were deco- rated with color. In this design, the Round Heel and Wedge Toe are worked with some two-color patterning and the rest of the color is added with duplicate stitch afterwards.

Materials: Renaissance Yarns' Froehlich-Wolle Special Blauband
(80% wool, 20% nylon, 50g/approx. 225 yards) #20 White, 2
skeins; #53 Turquoise, #58 Yellow, #10 Black, #73 Red, 1 skein
each or partial skeins.

Set of four #1 double-point needles or size to give gauge.

Gauge: 17 sts and 23 rounds = 2 inches in Stockinette stitch worked
in the round, before blocking.

LEG

CO 65 sts with White using the Continental method. Divide
the sts evenly onto 3 needles. Join into a round being careful not
to twist sts. This join marks the "seam line" and beginning of the
round.

K3 sts using both ends of the yarn. Drop the CO tail. *P2, k3;
repeat from *, ending p2.

Begin Lace Pattern:

Round 1: *YO, k2 tog, k1, p2; repeat from * to end of round.

Rounds 2 and 4: *K3, p2; repeat from * to end of round.

Round 3: *K1, SSK, YO, p2; repeat from * to end of round.

Repeat these 4 rounds 6 times more for a total of 7 repeats. On
last round, knit the last 2 purl sts together. 64 sts remain.

Continue even in Stockinette stitch until leg measures 8 inches total or desired length to heel flap.

Adjust sts so that there are 16 sts on needle #1, 32 sts on needle #2, and 16 sts on needle #3, and so that the "seam line" is between needles #1 and #3.

DIVIDE FOR HEEL

Knit across the first 16 sts on needle #1 with needle #3. There
are 32 sts on the heel needle and 32 sts on needle #2 to be held for
the instep. Turn the work.

Row 1: Sl1, p31. Turn.

Row 2: Sl1, k31. Turn.

Repeat these last two rows 5 more times for a total of 6 repeats.
End with Row 1 ready to begin a RS row (14 rows total). Continue following Heel Graph 1, beginning with row 15 (RS row). Continue to slip the first stitch of each row and knit the last stitch of
each row with Black. Work the last row of the heel flap, row 32
(WS row) with Red omitting the slipped stitch at the beginning of
the row, as shown on graph.

TURN HEEL

Continuing with Red, k18, SSK, k1, turn. Sl1, p5, p2 tog, p1,

Heel Graph 1

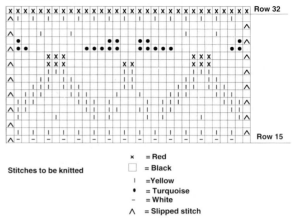

Row 32

Row 15

Stitches to be knitted

× = Red
□ = Black
I = Yellow
• = Turquoise
- = White
∧ = Slipped stitch

Heel Graph 2

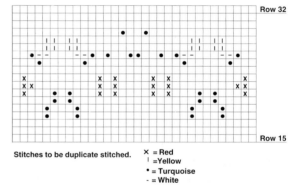

Row 32

Row 15

Stitches to be duplicate stitched.

× = Red
I = Yellow
• = Turquoise
- = White

turn. *Sl1, knit to within one stitch of the gap, SSK, k1, turn. Sl1,
purl to within one stitch of the gap, p2 tog, p1, turn. Repeat from
* until all sts are worked. End ready to begin a RS row. There are
18 heel sts. Knit to middle of heel (9 sts), break off Red, join White.

GUSSETS

Knit across 9 heel sts, pick up and k16 sts tbl along right side of
heel flap. With an empty needle, pick up and k1 st tbl at the beginning of the instep sts, work across the instep sts, pick up and k1
st tbl at the end of the instep sts. With an empty needle, pick up
and k16 sts tbl along left side of heel flap; then knit the first 9 sts
from the heel needle onto this last needle. There are 25 sts on needle #1, 34 instep sts on needle #2, and 25 sts on needle #3.

Referring to Heel Graph 2, add the duplicate sts to the heel flap
as indicated.

SHAPE GUSSET

Round 1: Work to 3 sts away from the end of needle #1, k2 tog, k1. SSK at the beginning of needle #2, work to 2 sts away from the end of needle #2, k2 tog. K1, SSK at the beginning of needle #3. Work to end of round. You will have 32 instep sts on needle #2.

Round 2: Work even in established pattern.

Round 3: Work decreases at the end of needle #1 and the beginning of needle #3. (Omit the decreases on the instep needle.)

Repeat these last two rounds until you have 16 sts each on needles #1 and #3, and 32 sts on needle #2. Continue in Stockinette stitch until foot length measures 3 3/4 inches less than desired length. Work Toe Graph 1 beginning as indicated. The last round of the pattern is a Red round.

Referring to Toe Graph 2, add in the duplicate stitches to the toe design as indicated.

SHAPE TOE

Round 1: With Red, work to 3 sts away from the end of needle #1; k2 tog, k1. K1, SSK at the beginning of needle #2; work to 3 sts from the end of needle #2; k2 tog, k1. K1, SSK at the beginning of needle #3. Work to end of round.

Round 2: Work even.

Repeat these last two rounds until you have 8 sts each on needles #1 and #3, and 16 sts on needle #2. Now work Round 1 (the decrease round) only until you have 4 sts each on needles #1 and #3, and 8 sts on needle #2. Knit across the sts on needle #1 with needle #3; this places the 8 back sts together onto one needle. Break yarn leaving a 10-inch tail. Kitchener stitch the two sets of 8 sts together to finish the toe.

Weave in ends. Block socks under a damp towel or on sock blockers.

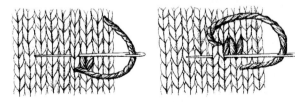

DUPLICATE STITCH. Bring needle through to the right side at the base of a stitch. Pass needle under both threads at the base of the stitch immediately above. Take needle through to the wrong side at the base of the first stitch and out at the base of the next stitch to be worked.

Toe Graph 1

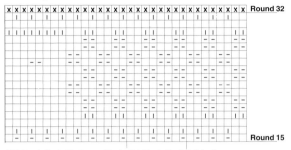

Stitches to be knitted   Begin right foot   Begin left foot

× = Red | = Yellow
☐ = Black   – = White

Toe Graph 2

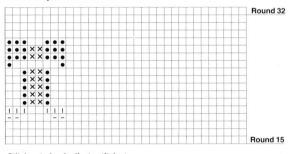

Stitches to be duplicate stitched

× = Red   • = Turquoise
| = Yellow   – = White

Greek Stockings, 19th century.

81

These socks were inspired by the fine lace stockings and socks knit throughout Europe and beyond during the eighteenth and nineteenth centuries. Many variations of this lace, which is related to the famous Shetland Feather and Fan pattern, show up on socks and stockings over and over again. This sock was adapted from one made of linen. It can be found in the Daughters of the American Revolution Museum in Washington, D.C. There was no date or maker's name available. It reminds us that the styles, ideas, and techniques that were created in Europe found their way to new lands and were carried on by knitters building a new life. These socks have a Round Heel shaping and a Wedge Toe finish. They are, of course, for ladies.

Materials: Brown Sheep Company's Wildfoote (75% washable wool, 25% nylon, 50g/approx. 215 yards) #Sy-10 Plain Vanilla, 2 skeins.

Set of four #000 (1.5mm) double-point needles or size to give gauge.

Gauge: 22 sts and 28 rounds = 2 inches over Stockinette stitch worked in the round.

LEG

CO 102 sts using the Continental method. Divide the sts evenly onto 3 needles. Join into a round being careful not to twist sts. This join marks the "seam line" and beginning of the round.

Scallop Lace Pattern (repeat of 17 sts)

Round 1: *K2, p13, k2; rep from *.

Round 2: Work as Round 1.

Round 3: *SSK, k13, k2 tog; rep from *.

Round 4: *SSK, k11, k2 tog; rep from *.

Round 5: *SSK, k9, k2 tog; rep from *.

Round 6: *SSK, k7, k2 tog; rep from *.

Round 7: *(K1, YO) 8 times, K1. Repeat from * 5 more times.

Repeat these 7 rounds of pattern 12 times total.

DIVIDE FOR HEEL

Sl1 as to knit, knit across next 50 sts. Place remaining 51 sts on another needle to be held for instep. Turn the work.

Row 1: Sl1 as to knit, p50 sts. Turn.

Row 2: Sl1 as to knit, k50 sts. Turn.

Repeat these last 2 rows 18 more times for a total of 19 repeats. End with Row 1, ready to begin a RS row (40 rows total).

TURN HEEL

Sl1 as to knit, k27, SSK, k1, turn. Sl1 as to purl, p6, p2 tog, p1, turn.

*Sl1 as to purl, knit to within one stitch of the gap, SSK, k1, turn. Sl1 as to purl, purl to within one stitch of the gap, p2 tog, p1, turn.

Repeat from * until all sts are worked. End ready to begin a RS row. There are 29 heel sts.

GUSSETS

Knit across 29 heel sts, pick up and k20 sts along right side of the heel flap. With an empty needle, work across the instep sts in pattern. With an empty needle pick up and k20 sts along left side of the heel flap; then knit the first 15 sts from the heel needle onto this last needle. Your round begins here. There are 34 sts on needle #1, 51 instep sts on needle #2, and 35 sts on needle #3.

SHAPE GUSSETS

Round 1: Knit to 3 sts away from the end of needle #1; k2 tog, k1. Pattern across the instep sts. K1, SSK at the beginning of needle #3. Knit to end of round.

Round 2: Work even in established patterns.

Repeat these two rounds 8 more times for a total of 9 repeats. There are 25 sts on needle #1, 51 instep sts on needle #2, and 26 sts on needle #3. Continue even in established patterns until foot measures approximately 2 inches less than desired length ending with Round 7 of pattern.

SHAPE TOE

Round 1: Knit to 3 sts away from the end of needle #1, k2 tog, k1. K1, SSK at the beginning of needle #2, knit to last 3 sts from end of needle #2, k2 tog, k1. K1, SSK at the beginning of needle #3. Knit to end of round.

Round 2: Work even.

Repeat these last two rounds until there are 13 sts on needle #1, 27 sts on needle #2, and 14 sts on needle #3. Now work Round 1 (the decrease round) only until there are 5 sts on needle #1, 11 sts on needle #2, and 6 sts on needle #3. Knit across the sts on needle #1 with needle #3; this places the 11 back sts together onto one needle. Break off yarn leaving a 10-inch tail. Kitchener stitch the two sets of 11 sts together to finish the toe.

Weave in ends. Block socks under a damp towel or on sock blockers.

While called Welsh Country Stockings, these could be named after a Highland glen, a Hebridean Isle, or a Yorkshire village. They represent the traditional stockings and socks made by hand knitters to clothe their families, to wear themselves, or to sell. I knit these stockings while on a journey in Wales. I was pleased when my hostess in a small inn came up to me and said "my mother used to knit stockings like yours". This design has shaping down the leg and a plain stockinette stitch heel flap. The heel is reinforced on the wrong side by weaving in the same yarn used in the heel, after the stocking was completed. The stockings have a Dutch Heel and Round Toe.

Materials: Brown Sheep Company's Nature Spun 3-ply Sport (100% wool, 100g/ approx. 368 yards) #N03 Grey Heather, #730 Natural, 1 skein each.

Set of four #1 double-point needles or size to give gauge.

Gauge: 16 sts and 22 rows = 2 inches over Stockinette stitch worked in the round.

LEG

CO 84 sts with Natural, alternating 2 sts cast on with the Continental method followed by 2 sts with the English method #2. Divide the sts evenly onto 3 needles. Join into a round being careful not to twist sts. This join marks the "seam line" and beginning of the round.

Using both ends of the yarn, k2, p2 sts. Drop the CO tail. *K2, p2; repeat from *.

Continue in k2, p2 ribbing as established for 1½ inches (16 rounds total). Change to Stockinette stitch. Work 25 more

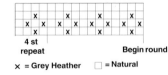

4 st repeat   **Begin round**

x = Grey Heather   ☐ = Natural

rounds. Join Grey Heather. Work 4 rounds of pattern from graph. Break Natural. Continue with Grey Heather. K5 rounds even.

LEG SHAPING

Round 1: K1, SSK. Work to 3 sts from end of round, k2 tog, k1.

Rounds 2-6: Work even.

Repeat these last 6 rounds 5 more times for a total of 6 repeats. 72 sts remain.

Continue even in Stockinette stitch until leg measures 10 inches total from CO edge. Break off Grey Heather.

Adjust the sts so that there are 18 sts on needle #1, 36 sts on needle #2, and 18 sts on needle #3, and so that the "seam line" is between needles #1 and #3.

DIVIDE FOR HEEL

Slip, as to purl, the first 18 sts on needle #1 onto needle #3. There are 36 sts on the heel needle, with the back "seam line" of the leg centered, and 36 sts on needle #2 to be held for instep. Attach Natural.

Row 1: With RS facing, k36 heel sts. Turn.

Row 2: K1 tbl, p34, sl1 wyf. Turn.

Row 3: K1 tbl, k34, sl1 wyf. Turn.

Repeat these last two rows 17 times more for a total of 18 re-

Knitted stockings from the Shetland Island, Foula.

peats. End with Row 2 ready to begin a RS row (36 rows total).

TURN HEEL

K23 , SSK, turn.

*Sl1, p10, p2 tog, turn. Sl1, k10, SSK, turn.

Repeat from * until all sts are worked. End ready to begin a RS row. There are 12 heel sts.

K6 heel sts. Break yarn, leaving an 8-inch tail. Attach Grey Heather and knit to end of heel sts, pick up and k18 sts tbl along right side of heel flap. With an empty needle, pick up and k1 st tbl at the beginning of the instep sts, knit instep sts, pick up and k1 st tbl at the end of the instep sts. With an empty needle, pick up and knit 18 sts tbl along left side of heel flap, then knit the first 6 sts from the heel needle onto this last needle. There are 24 sts on needle #1, 38 instep sts on needle #2, and 24 sts on needle #3, and the "seam line" is between needles #1 and #3.

SHAPE GUSSETS

Round 1: Knit to 2 sts away from the end of needle #1; k2 tog.

SSK at the beginning of the instep needle, knit to last 2 sts; k2 tog. SSK at the beginning of needle #3. Knit to end of round.

Round 2: Work even.

Round 3: Work decreases at the end of needle #1, and at the beginning of needle #3 only. (Omit the decreases on the instep needle.)

Repeat these last two rounds 5 more times for a total of 6 repeats. There are 18 sts on needles #1 and #3, and 36 instep sts on needle #2. Continue even until foot length measures $2\frac{1}{2}$ inches less than desired finished length. Break Grey Heather at the end of the last round. Attach Natural.

SHAPE TOE

Round 1: *K6, k2 tog; repeat from * around.

Rounds 2–7: Work even.

Round 8: *K5, k2 tog; repeat from * around.

Rounds 9–13: Work even.

Round 14: *K4, k2 tog; repeat from * around.

Rounds 15–18: Work even.

Continue in this manner working 1 less st, and 1 less plain round between each decrease round until there is 1 plain round only. K2 tog around. 9 sts remain. Break yarn leaving a 10-inch tail. Thread a blunt-point needle. Draw it through the remaining sts. Tighten up to finish the toe.

Weave in ends. Block socks under a damp towel or on sock blockers.

FINNISH SOCKS

*T*hese sporty socks are modeled after a pair of long stockings housed in the National Museum of Finland. The heel flap in these socks is reinforced with the heel stitch and this reinforcing continues into the Dutch Heel. The Double-Decrease Toe makes a narrow line on each side of the foot. These socks have unisex sizing. Add or subtract rows between the end of the ankle decreases and the beginning of the toe shaping to lengthen or shorten the leg and foot as needed.

Materials: Renaissance Yarns' Froehlich-Wolle Sedrun (90% wool, 10% nylon, 50g/approx. 131 yards) #5500 Cream, 2 skeins; #5509 Red, 1 skein.

Set of four #3 double-point needles or size to give gauge.

Gauge: 12 sts and 14 rounds = 2 inches over pattern worked in the round.

LEG

CO 50 sts with Cream using the English method. Divide the sts evenly onto 3 needles. Join into a round being careful not to twist sts. This join marks the "seam line" and beginning of the round.

Border Pattern:

Round 1: *P2, k3; rep from *.

Round 2: K1, *p2, k3; rep from *, end k2.

Round 3: K2, *p2, k3; rep from *, end k1.

Round 4: *K3, p2; rep from *.

Round 5: P1, *k3, p2; rep from * end p1.

Round 6: Same as Round 1.

Round 7: Same as Round 2.

Round 8: Same as Round 3.

K1 round, increasing 1 st at the beginning and 1 st at the end of the round. 52 sts total. K4 rounds. Attach Red. Work Graph A. K3 rounds with Cream. Work 3 repeats of Graph B. Break off Red. K1 round with Cream, decreasing 2 sts on the last round by knitting the 13th and 14th sts together and knitting the 39th and 40th sts together. Work to end of round. 50 sts remain.

Adjust sts so that there are 12 sts on needle #1, 25 sts on needle #2, and 13 sts on needle #3, and so that the "seam line" is between needles #1 and #3.

DIVIDE FOR HEEL

Knit across the first 11 sts on needle #1 with needle #3, sl1 wyf. There are 25 sts on the heel needle and 25 sts on needle #2 to be held for instep. Turn the work.

Row 1: K1 tbl, p23, sl1 wyf. Turn.

Row 2: K1 tbl, *k1, sl1 as to purl; repeat from * to last st, sl1 wyf. Turn.

Repeat these last two rows 12 more times for a total of 13 repeats. End with Row 1 ready to begin a RS row (26 rows total).

TURN HEEL

K16, k2 tog tbl, turn.

*Sl1, p7, p2 tog, turn. Sl1, (k1, sl1) 3 times, k1, k2 tog tbl. Repeat from * until all sts are worked. End ready to start RS row. There are 9 heel sts.

GUSSETS

*[Sl1, k1] 4 times, k1, pick up and k13 sts tbl along the right side of the heel flap. With an empty needle, pick up and k1 st tbl at the beginning of instep sts; work across the instep sts; pick up and k1 st tbl at the end of the instep sts. With an empty needle, pick up and k13 sts tbl along the left side of the heel flap; then knit the first 4 sts from the heel needle onto this last needle. You now have 18 sts on needle #1, 27 sts on needle #2, and 17 sts on needle #3.

SHAPE GUSSETS

Round 1: Knit to 3 sts away from the end of needle #1; k2 tog, k1. K2 tog tbl at the beginning of needle #2; work across instep sts in established pattern to last 2 sts, k2 tog. K1, k2 tog tbl at the beginning of needle #3. Knit to end of round.

Round 2: Work even in established pattern.

Round 3: Work decreases at the end of needle #1 and at the beginning of needle #3 only. (Omit the decreases on the instep needle.)

Repeat these last two rounds 3 more times for a total of 5 decreases. There are 13 sts on needle #1, 25 instep sts on needle #2, and 12 sts on needle #3. Work 1 round even. Attach Red and work Graph C. Work 6 rounds Cream. Repeat these 8 rounds once more. Work Graph C once. Break off Red. Work even until foot length measures 2¼ inches less than desired length from heel to toe.

SHAPE TOE

Round 1: Knit to 2 sts away from end of needle #1, sl 2 sts at the same time as if to knit, k1 from needle #2 onto the same needle and pass the 2 slipped stitches over the knitted st (this is a double decrease). Work across needle #2 to the last 2 sts, sl 2 sts at the same time as if to knit, k1 from needle #3 onto the same needle and pass the 2 slipped stitches over the knitted st. Knit to end of round.

Round 2: Work even in established pattern.

Repeat these last two rounds until there are 7 sts on needle #1, 13 sts on needle #2, and 6 sts on needle #3. Now work double decreases every round until a total of 6 sts remain. Break yarn leaving a 10-inch tail. Thread a blunt-point needle. Draw it through the remaining sts. Tighten up to finish the toe.

Weave in ends. Block socks under a damp towel or on sock blockers.

Graph A

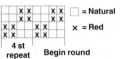

□ = Natural
× = Red

4 st repeat   Begin round

Graph B

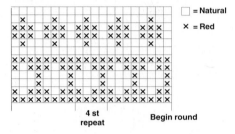

□ = Natural
× = Red

4 st repeat   Begin round

Graph C

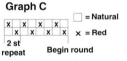

□ = Natural
× = Red

2 st repeat   Begin round

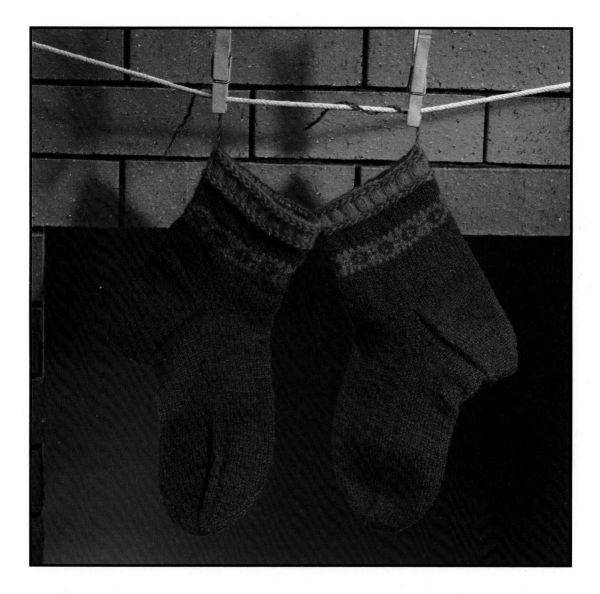

This pair of short socks was inspired by a collection of Estonian socks in the Nordeska Museum in Stockholm, Sweden. They are not dissimilar from snesokkar or "cut stockings" worn for festive occasions in Norway. The snesokkar were made with complex color and two-ended knitting techniques. They had a tassel at the toe that was used to hang the sock up to dry. These short socks have a bit longer leg than the snesokkar and two rows of braid separated by simple k2 p2 ribbing. The Shaped Common Heel has a good fit and the Star Toe finishes the foot. Rather than leaving a tassel at the toe where it was sure to cause some discomfort, the tassel is at the top, made from the remains of the cast-on yarns. This is a ladies' sock.

Materials: Nordic Fiber Arts' Raumagarn Finullgarn 2-ply (100% wool, 50g/approx. 178 yards) #488 Dark Cherry, 2 skeins; #435 Bright Red, #444 Dull Red, #427 Rose, #480 Burgundy,1 skein each (or leftovers of 4 other colors).

Set of 5 #0 double-point needles or size to give gauge.

Gauge: 15 sts and 22 rounds = 2 inches over Stockinette stitch worked in the round.

CO 72 sts with Dark Cherry over the index finger and Bright Red over the thumb using the Continental method. Do this by making a loop using both colors (loop doesn't figure in the total stitch count). Leave about 12 inches of each color beyond the loop to make the optional tassel later on. When all sts have been cast on, remove the loop made up of the two colors. Divide the sts evenly onto 3 needles (knit with needle #4—needle #5 will be used for the toe). Join into a round being careful not to twist sts. This join marks the "seam line" and beginning of the round.

LEG

Braid Pattern

Round 1:*K1 Dark Cherry, k1 Bright Red; repeat from * around.

Round 2: Bring both colors to the front of the work. Keep them in the same order as on previous round. *P1 Dark Cherry, p1 Bright Red, always bringing the next color to be used OVER the top of the last color used. Repeat from * around.

Round 3: *P1 Dark Cherry, p1 Bright Red, always bringing the next color to be used UNDER the last color used. Repeat from * around.

Round 4: Bring both colors to the back. Knit with Bright Red.

Rounds 5 to 9: With Bright Red, *k2, p2; repeat from *.

Round 10: Work as Round 1.

Round 11: Work as Round 2.

Round 12: Work as Round 3. Break off Bright Red.

Continuing with Dark Cherry, k9 rounds. Work Leg Pattern for 9 rounds according to graph. Break all colors except Dark Cherry. Continue to knit until leg measures 4 inches total.

Adjust the sts so that there are 18 sts on needle #1, 36 sts on needle #2, and 18 sts on needle #3, and so that the "seam line" is between needles #1 and #3.

DIVIDE FOR HEEL

Knit across the first 17 sts on needle #1 with needle #3, sl1 wyf. There are 36 sts on the heel needle and 36 sts on needle #2 to be

Leg Pattern

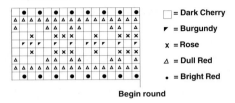

Begin round

held for instep. Turn.

Row 1: K1 tbl, p34, sl1 wyf. Turn.

Row 2: K1 tbl, k34, sl1 wyf. Turn.

Repeat these last two rows 18 more times for a total of 19 repeats. End with Row 1 ready to begin a RS row (38 rows total).

TURN HEEL

Row 1: K1 tbl, k15, k2 tog, place marker (M) SSK, k15, sl1 wyf.

Row 2: K1 tbl, purl to within one st from end of row, sl1 wyf.

Row 3: K1 tbl, knit to 2 sts before M, k2 tog, slip M, SSK, knit to within one st from end of row, sl1 wyf.

Row 4: Work as Round 2.

Repeat these last two rows 3 times more. Omit the sl1 wyf on last heel flap row. End ready to begin a RS row. There are 26 heel sts. Divide these 26 sts in half onto two needles. Break yarn leaving a 15-inch tail. Kitchener stitch the two sets of 13 sts together.

Beginning at the point under the heel at the Kitchener stitch join, pick up and k24 sts along right side of heel flap. With an empty needle, knit across the instep sts. With an empty needle, pick up and k24 sts along left side of heel. There are 24 sts on needle #1, 36 instep sts on needle #2, and 24 sts on needle #3.

SHAPE GUSSETS

Round 1: Knit to 3 sts away from the end of needle #1; k2 tog, k1. Knit across 36 instep sts. K1, SSK at the beginning of needle #3. Knit to end of round.

Round 2: Work even.

Repeat these two rounds 5 more times for a total of 6 repeats. There are 18 sts on needles #1 and #3, and 36 sts on needle #2. Work even on these 72 sts until foot length measures 2 inches less than desired finished length.

SHAPE TOE

Divide sts evenly onto 4 needles. Begin at needle #1.

Round 1: [K16, k2 tog] 4 times.

Round 2: Work even in established pattern.

Round 3: [Knit to last 2 sts from the end of the needle, k2 tog] 4 times.

Repeat these last two rounds until there are 9 sts on each needle. Now work Round 3 (decrease round) only until there are 2 sts on each needle. Break yarn leaving a 10-inch tail. Thread a blunt-point needle. Draw it through the remaining sts. Tighten up to finish the toe.

OPTIONAL TASSEL

Using the two ends which remain from the cast on, secure the finished sock by pinning it to a chair cushion or having it held by other helping hands. Hold one end of yarn in your right hand and one end in your left hand. Twist each end to the right with you fingers. As you do so, wrap them over each other to the left. When the tassel is the desired length, knot it together and cut off any excess yarn, leaving about an inch as fringe.

Weave in ends. Block socks under a damp towel or on sock blockers.

Estonian socks with tassels for hanging.

Generally the mention of Latvian knitting reminds us of colorful mittens. These socks were inspired, not by color knitting but by a pair of lacy Latvian stockings, knit in Latvia and owned by Lizbeth Upitis. The lace is simple to work and very decorative. The leg is shaped by working four decreases on one round midway down the leg. The heel is turned with Half-Handkerchief Heel shaping and the socks end with a Star Toe. These socks are sized for ladies.

Materials: Schoolhouse Yarns' Helmi Vuorelma Oy Satakieli 2-ply (100% wool, 100g/ approx. 357 yards) #003 Natural, 1 skein. Set of five #0 double-point needles.

These socks took almost every inch of the yarn called for. If you need to make a longer foot, omit one repeat of the lace on the leg or have more yarn available.

Gauge: 18 sts and 25 rounds = 2 inches over Stockinette stitch worked in the round.

19 sts and 24 rounds = 2 inches over lace pattern worked in the round.

LEG

CO 76 sts using the Continental method. Divide the sts evenly onto 3 needles (knit with needle #4—needle #5 will be used for the foot). Join into a round being careful not to twist sts. This join marks the "seam line" and beginning of the round.

Work 7 rounds in Stockinette stitch. Work one round of Picot Pattern: *k2 tog, YO; repeat from *. Work 7 more rounds in Stockinette stitch. Join hem as follows: With another double-point needle, pick up 1 st along cast-on edge for every st cast on; knit each st with its corresponding live st on the needle. (It is easiest to pick up 1 st at a time and knit it with its corresponding live st before moving on to the next st.) OR: Cast on invisibly using waste yarn. Join the two edges by removing the waste yarn and knitting the resulting live sts with the sts on the needle. This will turn the hem up and attach it to the body of the work. The Picot Pattern makes a decorative turning row.

Work one round even in Stockinette stitch then begin the Lace Pattern.

LACE PATTERN

Round 1: *P2, k5, k2 tog, YO, k1, YO, SSK, k5, p2. Repeat from *.
Round 2 and all even rounds: *P2, k15, p2. Repeat from *.
Round 3: *P2, k4, k2 tog, YO, k3, YO, SSK, k4, p2. Repeat from *.
Round 5: *P2, k3, k2 tog, YO, k5, YO, SSK, k3, p2. Repeat from *.
Round 7: *P2, k2, k2 tog, YO, k7, YO, SSK, k2, p2. Repeat from *.
Round 9: *P2, k1, k2 tog, YO, k9, YO, SSK, k1, p2. Repeat from *.
Repeat these 10 rounds 5 more times for a total of 6 repeats. Begin shaping on Round 10 of the 6th repeat.

SHAPE CALF

*P2, k15, p1, p2 tog, p1. Repeat from * around to last st. Work last st and first st as p2 tog. 72 sts remain.

Continue in newly established pattern working p3 between each lace panel instead of p4. Work 4 more repeats for a total of 10 repeats of the lace pattern.

Adjust the sts so that there are 18 sts on needle #1, 35 sts on needle #2, and 19 sts on needle #3, and so that the "seam line" is between needles #1 and #3.

DIVIDE FOR HEEL

Knit across the first 17 sts on needle #1 with needle #3, sl1 wyf. There are 37 sts on the heel needle, and 35 sts on needle #2 to be held for instep. There are 2 lace pattern repeats on needle #2 with one purl st at the beginning, one at the end, and three in the center. Turn the work.

Row 1: K1 tbl, p35, sl1 wyf. Turn.
Row 2: K1 tbl, *k1, sl1 as to purl; repeat from *, ending k1, sl1 wyf. Turn.

Repeat these last two rows 18 more times for a total of 19 repeats. End with Row 1 ready to begin a RS row (38 rows total).

Latvian stockings.

TURN HEEL

K1 tbl, k18, k2 tog tbl, k1. Turn. Sl1 as to purl, p2, p2 tog, p1. Turn. *Sl1 as to purl, knit to within one st of the gap, k2 tog tbl, k1, turn. Sl1 as to purl, purl to one st before the gap, p2 tog, p1, turn. Repeat from * until all sts are worked. There are 19 heel sts.

GUSSETS

Sl1 as to purl, k18 heel sts, pick up and k18 sts along right side of heel flap. With an empty needle, pick up and k1 st tbl at the beginning of the instep sts; work across the instep sts in established pattern (Round 1 of Lace Pattern); pick up and k1 st tbl at the end of the instep sts. With an empty needle, pick up and k18 sts along left side of heel flap; then knit the first 9 sts from the heel needle onto this last needle. There are 28 sts on needle #1, 37 instep sts on needle #2, and 27 sts on needle #3.

SHAPE GUSSETS

Round 1 (begins at center back heel): Knit to 3 sts away from the end of needle #1; k2 tog, k1. P2 tog at the beginning of needle #2; work across instep sts in established pattern to last 2 sts; p2 tog. K1, SSK at the beginning of needle #3. Work to end of round.

Round 2: Work even in established pattern.

Round 3: Work decreases at the end of needle #1, and at the beginning of needle #3 only. (Omit the decreases on the instep needle.)

Repeat these last two rounds a total of 8 times. 72 sts remain. There are 19 sts on needle #1, 35 instep sts on needle #2, and 18 sts on needle #3. Continue even in established pattern until there are 6 repeats of the lace pattern on the foot.

Divide sts onto 4 needles with 18 sts on each needle by placing the last st on needle #1 onto needle #2 and split the sts on needle #2 onto two needles. Continue in Stockinette stitch until foot length measures 2 inches less than desired finished length.

SHAPE TOE

Round 1: K2 tog at end of each needle (4 sts decreased).
Round 2: Work even.

Repeat these last two rounds 6 times total. 12 sts on each needle. Now work Round 1 (the decrease round) only until there are 2 sts on each needle. Break yarn leaving a 10-inch tail. Thread a blunt-point needle. Draw it through the remaining sts. Tighten up to finish off.

Weave in the end. Block socks under a damp towel or on sock blockers.

HIGHLAND SCHOTTISCHE KILT HOSE

T*he Highland Schottische is a step found in Scottish Country Dancing. It is a traveling step used when dancing to a strathspey tempo. This step has elegant movements and is a joy to do as well as to watch. These Kilt Hose also have an elegance about them. The pattern in the top is reflective of argyle patterns, with diamond shapes and crossing lines. The rib-like leg pattern is made up of curving lines of stitches combined with lacy holes to give a fancy design. The heel flap is reinforced with slipped stitches and the shaping is a Round Heel. The toe shaping is the longer variation of a Wedge Toe. These hose are sized for men.*

Materials: Brown Sheep Company's Nature Spun 3-ply Sport (100% wool, 100g/approx. 368 yards) #720 Ash, 2 skeins.
Set of four #2 double-point needles or size to give gauge.
Gauge: 16 sts and 20 rounds = 2 inches over Stockinette stitch worked in the round.

TURN-DOWN CUFF

CO 78 sts using the Continental Method. Divide the sts evenly onto 3 needles. Join into a round being careful not to twist sts. This join marks the "seam line" and beginning of the round.

K5 rounds. Work one round in Picot Pattern: *K2 tog, YO; repeat from * around. K5 more rounds. Join hem as follows: With another double-point needle, pick up 1 st along cast-on edge for every stitch cast on and knit each stitch together with its corresponding live stitch on the needle. (It is easiest to pick up 1 st at a time and knit it together with its corresponding live st before moving on to the next st.) OR: Cast on invisibly using waste yarn. Join the two edges by removing the waste yarn and knitting the resulting live sts with the sts on the needle. This will turn the hem up and attach it to the body of the work. The Picot Pattern makes a decorative turning row.

Work 2 repeats of Cuff graph (36 rounds).

LEG

K1 round. P1 round. K1 round. On next round, decrease as follows *k5, k2 tog, repeat from *, ending k8. 68 sts remain. Work k1,

p1 ribbing for 2½ inches total. On last rib round, increase 13 sts evenly spaced. 81 sts total.

At this point, turn the work inside out. There is a slight hole where you turned the work and reversed the knitting direction. This is normal and will be hidden by the turned-down cuff.

Adjust sts on your needles so you have 26 sts on needle #1, 31 sts on needle #2, and 24 sts on needle #3.

SHAPE CALF

Begin working leg pattern according to graph. Work leg pattern for 2 inches. Work decreases as follows: Work first 3 sts of round, SSK, (this SSK comes right after the first purl st of the round); work in established pattern to last 3 sts of round; k2 tog, p last st. Repeat this decrease every 6th round 8 more times for a total of 9 repeats. 63 sts remain. There are 17 sts on needle #1, 31 sts on needle #2, and 15 sts on needle #3, and the "seam line" is between needles #1 and #3.

Continue even on these sts in established pattern until leg measures 14 inches or desired length from purl round at the top of sock.

DIVIDE FOR HEEL

Knit across 17 sts on needle #1 with needle #3. There are 32 sts on the heel needle and 31 sts on needle #2 to be held for instep. Turn work.

Row 1: Sl1, p31. Turn.

Row 2: *Sl1, k1; repeat from * across row. Turn.

Row 3: Sl1, p 31. Turn.

Repeat these last 2 rows 15 times more for a total of 16 repeats. End with Row 3 ready to begin a RS row (32 rows total).

TURN HEEL

K18, SSK, k1, turn.

Sl1, p5, p2 tog, p1, turn.

*Sl1, knit to within one stitch of the gap, SSK, k1, turn. Sl1, purl to within one stitch of the gap, p2 tog, p1, turn. Repeat from * until all sts are worked. End ready to begin a RS row. There are 18 heel sts.

GUSSETS

Knit across 18 heel sts, pick up and k16 sts tbl along right side of the heel flap. With an empty needle, work across the instep sts in established pattern. With an empty needle, pick up and k16 sts tbl along left side of the heel flap; then knit the first 9 sts from heel needle onto this last needle. There are 25 sts on needle #1, 31 instep sts on needle #2, and 25 sts on needle #3.

SHAPE GUSSETS

Round 1: Knit to 3 sts away from end of needle #1; k2 tog, k1. Work across instep sts in established pattern. K1, SSK at the beginning of needle #3. Work to end of round. Round 2: Work even in established pattern.

Repeat these last two rounds 8 more times for a total of 9 repeats. There are 16 sts each on needles #1 and #3, and 31 instep sts on needle #2. Continue even in established pattern until foot length measures 2½ inches less than desired length. End having worked Round 3 of Leg Pattern. K1 round, increasing 1 st at the beginning of needle #2. There are 32 instep sts. Discontinue leg pattern.

SHAPE TOE

Round 1: Knit to 3 sts away from the end of needle #1; k2 tog, k1. K1, SSK at the beginning of needle #2; work to 3 sts away from the end of needle #2; k2 tog, k1. K1, SSK at the beginning of needle #3. Knit to end of round.

Round 2: Work even.

Repeat these last two rounds until you have 4 sts each on needles #1 and #3, and 8 sts on needle #2. Knit across the sts on needle #1 with needle #3; this places the 8 back sts together onto one needle. Break yarn leaving a 10-inch tail. Kitchener stitch the two sets of 8 sts together to finish the toe.

Weave in ends. Fold top at purl round. Block stockings under a damp towel or on sock blockers.

Cuff

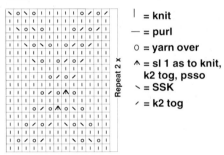

| = knit

— = purl

o = yarn over

∧ = sl 1 as to knit, k2 tog, psso

╲ = SSK

╱ = k2 tog

Repeat 2 x

Leg Pattern

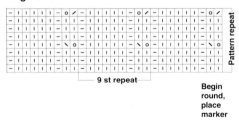

9 st repeat

Pattern repeat

Begin round, place marker

Traveling twisted stitches have been used to decorate stockings from Bavaria, Tyrol, Alsace, and Norway. Traveling stitch clocks can be found on Danish and Estonian stockings. The pattern here takes elements from a number of stockings with traveling stitches, yet has a Bavarian flavor. The traveling stitches begin several rounds below the end of the ribbing or welt and there is a decorated seam running down the back of the leg. The heel shaping is a Half-Handkerchief Heel and the toe is the longer version of the Wedge Toe. This pair of socks is sized for a lady. For man's socks, go up a needle size and work more Stockinette stitch rounds in the foot to add length before the toe shaping begins.

Leg Pattern

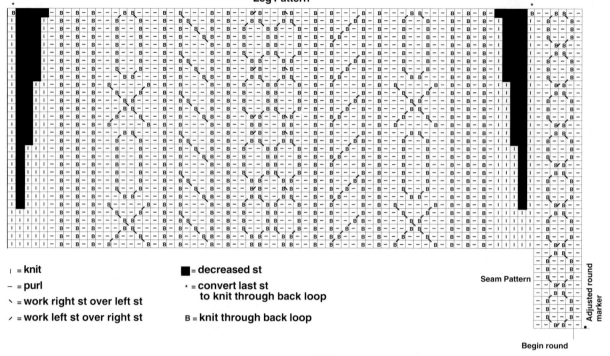

Seam Pattern

Adjusted round marker

Begin round

| = knit

− = purl

\ = work right st over left st

⁄ = work left st over right st

■ = decreased st

∗ = convert last st to knit through back loop

B = knit through back loop

For a detailed explanation on how to read these graphs, see "Key to Reading Traveling Stitch Graphs," page 100.

Instep Pattern

Repeat

Materials: Berroco's Wendy Guernsey 5-ply (100% wool, 100g/approx. 245 yards) #590 Bright Red, 2 skeins.

Set of four #1 double-point needles or size to give gauge.

Gauge: 15 sts and 21 rounds = 2 inches over Stockinette stitch worked in the round.

LEG

CO 72 sts using the Continental method. Divide the sts evenly onto 3 needles. Join into a round being careful not to twist sts. This join marks the "seam line" and beginning of the round.

Rounds 1–12: *P2, k2; repeat from * to last 2 sts, end k2.

Rounds 13–22: Begin Seam Pattern as shown on graph: *Work 6 sts of Seam Pattern, k66 sts. Repeat from * 9 times more.

SHAPE CALF

Begin working leg pattern according to graph. On the 6th round of the leg pattern, decrease as follows: Work first 7 sts of round, SSK, work in established pattern to last 3 sts of round, k2 tog, k1. Repeat these decreases every 8 rounds 3 more times for a total of 4 repeats. The plain knit sts remaining (on either side of the seam pattern) after the decreases are complete are converted to k tbl for the remainder of the leg pattern. Knit to end of round. 64 sts remain.

Continue even in established patterns until leg measures approximately 8 inches total, and the center 64 sts of the leg graph have been repeated once more. On the last round, work first 3 sts on needle #1 onto needle #3 to center the Seam Pattern along the back of the leg.

Adjust the sts so that there are 16 sts on needle #1, 32 sts on needle #2, and 16 sts on needle #3, and so that the "seam line" is between needles #1 and #3.

DIVIDE FOR HEEL

Knit across the first 15 sts on needle #1 with needle #3, sl1 wyf. There are 32 sts on the heel needle, and 32 sts on needle #2 to be held for instep. Turn the work.

Row 1: K1 tbl, p30, sl1 wyf. Turn.

Row 2: K1 tbl, k30, sl1 wyf. Turn.

Repeat these last two rows 15 more times for a total of 16 repeats. End with Row 1 ready to begin a RS row (32 rows total).

TURN HEEL

K16, k2 tog tbl, k1, turn. Sl1, p1, p2 tog, p1, turn.

*Sl1, knit to within one stitch of the gap, k2 tog tbl, k1, turn. Sl1, purl to within one stitch of the gap, p2 tog, p1, turn. Repeat from * until all sts are worked. End ready to begin a RS row. There are 16 heel sts.

GUSSETS

Knit across 16 heel sts, pick up and k16 sts tbl along right side of the heel flap. With an empty needle, pick up and k1 st tbl at the beginning of the instep sts; work across the instep sts in pattern following the instep graph; pick up and k1 st tbl at the end of the instep sts. With an empty needle, pick up and k16 sts tbl along left side of the heel flap; then knit the first 8 sts from the heel needle onto this last needle. There are 24 sts on needle #1, 34 instep sts on needle #2, and 24 sts on needle #3.

SHAPE GUSSETS

Round 1: Knit to 3 sts away from the end of needle #1; k2 tog, k1. P2 tog at the beginning of the instep needle; work across instep sts in established pattern to last 2 sts; p2 tog. K1, SSK at the beginning of needle #3. Knit to end of round.

Round 2: Work even in established patterns.

Round 3: Work decreases at the end of needle #1 and at the beginning of needle #3 only. (Omit the decreases on the instep needle.)

Repeat these last two rounds 6 more times for a total of 7 repeats. There are 16 sts on needles #1 and #3, and 32 instep sts on needle #2. Continue even in established pattern for a total of 3 repeats of the instep graph. Change to Stockinette stitch. Work even until foot length measures approximately 2¼ inches less than desired finished length.

SHAPE TOE

Round 1: Knit to 3 sts away from the end of needle #1; k2 tog, k1. K1, SSK at the beginning of needle #2; knit to last 3 sts from the end of needle #2; k2 tog, k1. K1, SSK at the beginning of needle #3. Knit to end of round.

Round 2: Work even in established pattern.

Repeat these last two rounds until there are 8 sts each on needles #1 and #3, and 16 sts on needle #2. Now work Round 1 (the decrease round) only until there are 4 sts each on needles #1 and #3, and 8 sts on needle #2. Knit across the sts on needle #1 with needle #3. This places the 8 back sts together onto one needle. Break yarn leaving a 10-inch tail. Kitchener stitch the two sets of 8 sts together to finish the toe.

Weave in ends. Block socks under a damp towel or on sock blockers.

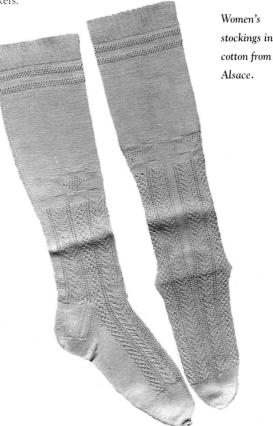

Women's stockings in cotton from Alsace.

Key to Reading the Traveling Stitch Graphs

Adapted from Lisl Fanderl's books and the description of the notations made by Kim Hughes to accompany them. The following explanation describes how to work the traveling stitches depicted in the graphs for the Chalet Socks (p. 97) and the Estonian Socks (p. 101).

 Cross the left st behind the right st: Sl2 sts onto the right-hand needle. With left-hand needle in front of work, going from left to right, skip the nearest slipped st and place the needle into the next slipped st. Remove the right-hand needle from both slipped sts, allowing the st you skipped to be off the needle for a moment. Now pick up this free st from the back with the right-hand needle and place it on the left-hand needle. Knit each st tbl.

 Cross the left st in front of the right st: Sl2 sts onto the right-hand needle. With left-hand needle behind work, going from left to right, skip the nearest slipped st and place the needle into the next slipped st. Remove the right-hand needle from both slipped sts, allowing the st you skipped to be off the needle for a moment. Now pick up this free st from the front with the right-hand needle and place it on the left-hand needle. Knit each st tbl.

 Cross the k tbl st in front of the purl st to the right: Sl a purl st and a k tbl st onto the right-hand needle. With the left-hand needle behind the work, going from left to right, skip the k tbl st and place the needle in the purl st. Remove the right-hand needle from both slipped sts, allowing the k tbl st you skipped to be off the needle for a moment. Now pick up this free st from the front with the right-hand needle and place it on the left-hand needle. Now k1 tbl, p1.

Cross the k tbl st in front of the purl st to the left: Sl a k tbl st and a purl st onto the right-hand needle. With the left-hand needle in front of the work, going from left to right, skip the purl st and place the needle in the k tbl st. Remove the right-hand needle from both slipped sts, allowing the purl st you skipped to be off the needle for a moment. Now pick up this free stitch from the back with the right-hand needle and place it on the left-hand needle. Now p1, k1 tbl.

Cross the k tbl st in front of the purl st to the right and make a knit out of the purl: Sl a purl st and a k tbl st onto the right-hand needle. With the left-hand needle behind the work, going from left to right, skip the k tbl st and place the needle in the purl st. Remove the right-hand needle from both slipped sts, allowing the k tbl st you skipped to be off the needle for a moment. Now pick up this free st from the front with the right-hand needle and place it on the left-hand needle. Now k1 tbl, k1 tbl.

 Cross the k tbl st in front of the purl st to the left and make a knit out of the purl: Sl a k tbl st and a purl st onto the right-hand needle. With the left-hand needle in front of the work, going from left to right, skip the purl st and place the needle in the k tbl st. Remove the right-hand needle from both slipped sts, allowing the k tbl st you skipped to be off the needle for a moment. Now pick up this free st from the back with the right-hand needle and place it on the left-hand needle. Now k1 tbl, k1 tbl.

The inspiration for these interesting socks is taken from a lady's sock made on the Estonian island of Kihnu. This sock dates from the second half of the nineteenth century. The original is in the Estonian National Museum in Tartu. The patterned top used in the following pattern was adapted from a book on Estonian costume. The leg clock patterns are identical to the museum piece. They have a twisted traveling stitch braid on one side and blocks of twisted stitches on the other. These socks have a Band Heel and a Wedge Toe. There is no gusset shaping. They are sized for a lady.

Cuff Pattern

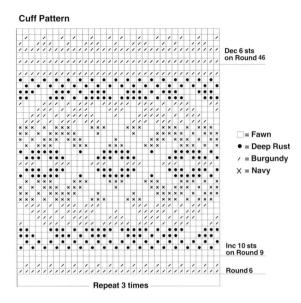

Dec 6 sts
on Round 46

Inc 10 sts
on Round 9

Round 6

☐ = Fawn
● = Deep Rust
╱ = Burgundy
✕ = Navy

Repeat 3 times

Clock Patterns

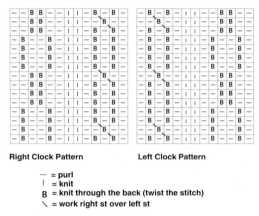

Right Clock Pattern   **Left Clock Pattern**

— = purl
| = knit
B = knit through the back (twist the stitch)
╲ = work right st over left st

For a detailed explanation on how to read this graph, see "Key to Reading Traveling Stitch Graphs," page 100.

Materials: Nordic Fiber Arts' Rauma Finullgarn 2-ply (100% wool, 50g/approx. 178 yards) #452 Fawn, 2 skeins; #444 Deep Rust, #480 Burgundy, #449 Navy, 1 skein each.

Set of four #0 double-point needles or size to give gauge.

Gauge: 15 sts and 22 rounds = 2 inches over Stockinette stitch worked in the round.

18 sts and 20 rounds = 2 inches over color patterning worked in the round.

LEG

CO 92 sts with Fawn over the index finger and Burgundy over the thumb using the Continental method. Divide the sts evenly onto 3 needles. Join into a round being careful not to twist sts. This join marks the "seam line" and beginning of the round.

Round 1: Purl with Fawn.

Round 2: Knit with Burgundy.

Round 3: Purl with Burgundy.

Round 4: Knit with Fawn.

Round 5: Purl with Fawn.

Begin working pattern for cuff according to graph. Rnds 6–8: Work 2 repeats of stitches as shown, then work 24 sts more following chart to complete rnd—92 sts.

Rnd 9: Increase 10 sts evenly spaced—102 sts.

Rnds 11–45: Repeat 34 motif sts 3 times each rnd.

Rnd 46: Decrease 6 sts evenly spaced—96 sts. Cut all contrast colors, continue with Fawn.

Increase and decrease stitches evenly spaced on rounds 9 and 41 as indicated on graph. Work graph to end. 96 sts total. Cut all contrast colors. Continue with Fawn.

Begin clock patterns at sides

Round 1: K22, work Right Clock Pattern according to graph over next 13 sts. Knit next 26 sts. Work Left Clock Pattern over next 13 sts, k22 sts.

Rounds 2 & 3: Work even in established patterns.

SHAPE CALF

Round 4: *K1, SSK, k19 sts, work across 13 clock sts as established, k26 sts, work across 13 clock sts as established, k19 sts, k2 tog, k1. Repeat from * every 6th round 7 more times for a total of 8 repeats. Knit to end of round. 80 sts remain.

Continue even in established patterns until you have 9 twisted cable crossings from the beginning of the Clock Patterns. Work 1 more round in pattern.

Adjust the sts so that there are 20 sts on needle #1, 40 sts on needle #2, and 20 sts on needle #3, and so that the "seam line" is between needles #1 and #3.

DIVIDE FOR HEEL

Work in patt across the 20 sts on needle #1 with needle #3. Break yarn. There are now 40 heel sts on needle #3, and 40 sts on needle #2 to be held for instep. The division between these two sets of 40 sts will be between the two knit sts that separate the two sections of the clock pattern.

Note: When working the reverse side of the heel, keep in established pattern. Knit the knit sts, purl the cable purl sts through the back loop. Move sts on the wrong side of the work to complete the traveling stitch cable as established.

Row 1: With right side facing, join yarn. K1 tbl, work 5 sts in cable half of Clock Pattern, K28 , work 5 sts in cable half of Clock Pattern, sl1 wyf. Turn.

Row 2: K1 tbl, work 5 sts of cable pattern, p28, work 5 sts of cable pattern, sl1 wyf. Turn.

Repeat these last two rows 11 more times for a total of 12 repeats. End with Row 2 ready to begin a RS row (24 rows total).

Row 1: K1 tbl, work 5 sts of cable pattern, k9, k2 tog, k6, SSK, k9, work 5 sts of cable pattern, sl1 wyf, turn.

Row 2: Work even in established pattern, turn.

Row 3: K1 tbl, work 5 sts of cable pattern, k8, k2 tog, k6, SSK, k8, work 5 sts of cable pattern, sl1 wyf, turn. Continue decreasing in this manner 4 times total — 32 sts rem. AT THE SAME TIME, continue cable pattern until you have 13 cable twists in all plus 4 more rows. Discontinue cable pattern.

TURN HEEL

K1 tbl, k18, SSK, turn. Sl1, p6, p2 tog, turn.

*Sl1, k6, SSK, turn. Sl1, p6, p2 tog, turn. Repeat from * until all sts are worked. End ready to begin a RS row. There are 8 heel sts.

GUSSETS

K across 8 heel sts, pick up and k16 sts tbl along right side of the heel flap. With an empty needle, work across the instep sts in established pattern. With an empty needle, pick up and k16 sts tbl along left side of the heel flap; then knit the first 4 sts from the heel needle onto this last needle. There are 20 sts on needle #1, 40 instep sts on needle #2, and 20 sts on needle #3.

Continue working circularly in established patterns until you have 12½ repeats of the "block" part of the clock pattern. End Clock Pattern. Continue in Stockinette stitch until foot length measures 2½ inches less that desired finished length.

SHAPE TOE

Round 1: Knit to 3 sts away from the end of needle #1; k2 tog, k1. K1, SSK at the beginning of needle #2; knit to 3 sts away from the end needle #2, k2 tog, k1. K1, SSK at the beginning of needle #3. K to end of round.

Round 2: Work even in established pattern.

Repeat these last two rounds until you have 10 sts each on needles #1 and #3, and 20 sts on needle #2. Now work Round 1 (the decrease round) only until you have 4 sts each on needles #1 and #3, and 8 sts on needle #2. Knit across the sts on needle #1 with needle #3, placing the 8 back sts together onto one needle. Break yarn leaving a 10-inch tail. Kitchener stitch the two sets of 8 sts together to finish the toe.

Weave in ends. Block socks under a damp towel or on sock blockers.

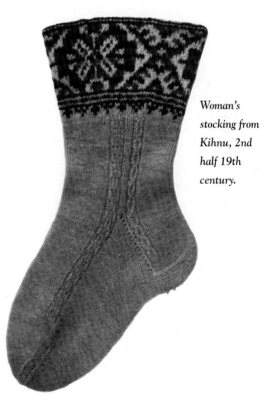

Woman's stocking from Kihnu, 2nd half 19th century.

LITHUANIAN AMBER SOCKS

The design for these socks comes directly from a photograph of an undated pair of socks in the National Museum of Lithuania in Vilnius. They are made of black and natural grey wool. The inspiration for amber yarn used as the main color in this design comes from the precious fossil resin, amber, found along the Baltic coastline. These socks will fit a small lady's foot.

To enlarge, go up a needle size. They have a Dutch Heel and a Wedge Toe.

Materials: Renaissance Yarns' Froehlich-Wolle Sedrun 5-ply (90% wool, 10% nylon, 50g/approx. 131 yards) #5562 Amber, 2 skeins; #5510 Black, 1 skein.

Set of four #4 double-point needles or size to give gauge.

Gauge: 12 sts and 14 rounds = 2 inches over pattern worked in the round, before blocking.

LEG

CO 44 sts with Amber using the Continental method. Divide the sts evenly onto 3 needles. Join into a round being careful not to twist sts. This join marks the "seam line" and beginning of the round.

Round 1: *K2, p2; repeat from * around for 2½ inches total. Change to Black. Work pattern according to graph. When last Black round is complete, break both yarns.

DIVIDE FOR HEEL

Place the first 10 sts and the last 11 sts of the round onto one needle for the heel. Place remaining 23 sts onto another needle for the instep.

Row 1: With RS facing, join both colors. *K1 Amber, k1 Black. Repeat from * ending k1 Amber. Turn.

Row 2: *P1 Amber, p1 Black. Repeat from * ending p1 Amber. Turn.

Repeat these last two rows 7 more times for a total of 8 repeats. End with Row 2 ready to begin a RS row (16 rows total).

TURN HEEL

[K1 Amber, k1 Black] 6 times, k1 Amber, k2 tog tbl with Black, turn.

*Sl1 as to purl, [p1 Amber, p1 Black] 2 times, p1 Amber, p2 tog with Black, turn. Sl1 as to purl, [k1 Amber, k1 Black] 2 times, k1 Amber, k2 tog tbl with Black. Turn. Repeat from * until all sts are worked. End ready to begin a RS row. There are 7 heel sts.

GUSSETS

Work across 7 heel sts as follows: Sl1, k1 Amber, k1 Black, k4 Amber; with Amber, pick up and knit 11 sts along right side of the heel flap. With an empty needle, pick up and k1 st tbl at the beginning of the instep sts; work across the 23 instep sts in pattern following the foot graph. With an empty needle, pick up and k12 sts along left side of the heel flap; then knit the first 3 sts from the heel needle onto this last needle. There are 15 sts on needle #1, 24 sts on needle #2, and 15 sts on needle #3.

SHAPE GUSSETS

Round 1, Needle #1: [K3 Amber, k1 Black] 2 times, k4 Amber, k2 tog with Amber, k1 Amber. Needle #2: SSK with Black, [k3

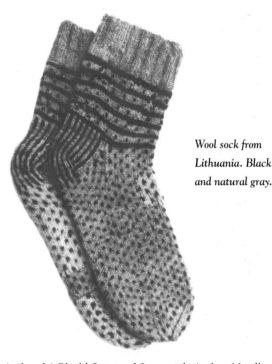

Wool sock from Lithuania. Black and natural gray.

Amber, k1 Black] 5 times, k2 tog with Amber. Needle #3: K1 Amber, SSK with Amber, [k3 Amber, k1 Black] 3 times.

Round 2: Work even with Amber.

Round 3, Needle #1: K1 Amber, k1 Black, [k3 Amber, k1 Black] 2 times, k1 Amber, k2 tog with Amber, k1 Amber. Needle #2: K2 Amber, [k1 Black, k3 Amber] 5 times. Needle #3: K1 Amber, SSK with Amber, [k1 Black, k3 Amber] 2 times, k1 Black, k2 Amber.

Round 4: Work even with Amber.

Continue in this manner following Foot Pattern and work [k2 tog with Amber, k1 Amber, at the end of needle #1, and k1 Amber, SSK with Amber at the beginning of needle #3] every pattern round 2 more times. There are 11 sts each on needles #1 and #3, and 22 instep sts on needle #2. Continue even in established pattern. Work even until foot length measures 2 inches less than desired finished length. End having worked a plain Amber round.

SHAPE TOE

Round 1: With Black, knit to 3 sts away from the end of needle #1; k2 tog, k1. K1, SSK at the beginning of needle #2; work to last 3 sts from the end of needle #2; k2 tog, k1. K1, SSK at the beginning of needle #3. Work to end of round.

Round 2: Work even with Amber.

Repeat these last two rounds until there are 5 sts each on needles #1 and #3, and 10 sts on needle #2. Continuing in striped pattern, work Round 1 (the decrease round) only until there are 2 sts on needles #1 and #3, and 4 sts on needle #2. Break yarn leaving a 10-inch tail. Thread a blunt-point needle. Draw it through the remaining sts. Tighten up to finish the toe.

Weave in ends. Block socks under a damp towel or on sock blockers.

Leg Pattern

□ = Amber
× = Black

Foot Pattern

□ = Amber
× = Black

Fair Isle Sock

SHETLAND SOCKS

These Fair Isle patterned socks are worked in the colors of the land that inspired them: heather, moss, and peaty earth. The top is, in a way, a tiny Fair Isle sampler, with corrugated ribbing at the beginning, a peerie pattern, and then a traditional X-and-O pattern all worked in three shades of two hues of rust and green. There is a Band Heel with no gussets. A Round Toe shaping finishes off the foot. These socks are designed for women.

Materials: Jamieson and Smith's Shetland Jumper Weight 2-ply (100% wool, 1 ounce/approx. 150 yards) #1295 Dark Green, 2 skeins. 1 skein of each of the following colors: #1293 Medium Green, #FC24 Light Green, #FC44 Dark Rust, #122 Medium Rust, #32 Light Rust.

Set of five #1 double-point needles or size to give gauge.

Gauge: 18 sts and 22 rounds = 2 inches over Fair Isle pattern worked in the round.

16 sts and 24 rounds = 2 inches over Stockinette stitch worked in the round.

TURN-DOWN CUFF

CO 90 sts with Dark Green using the Continental method. Divide the sts evenly onto 3 needles (knit with needle #4—needle #5 will be used for the foot). Join into a round being careful not to twist sts. This join marks the "seam line" and beginning of the round.

Round 1: *K2 Medium Rust, p3 Dark Green. Repeat from * to end of round. Work Round 1 for 4 rounds total.

Begin working cuff pattern according to graph. When graph is complete, break all yarns except Dark Green. K3 rounds, p1 round, k2 rounds.

On next round, decrease as follows: *k7, k2 tog, repeat from * to end of round. 80 sts remain. Knit 3 rounds with Dark Green. Work k2, p2 ribbing for 2 inches total.

At this point, turn the work inside out. Continue in circular Stockinette stitch until top measures 7¼ inches total from cast-on edge. There is a slight hole where you turned the work and reversed knitting direction. This is normal and will be hidden by the turned-down cuff.

Adjust the sts so that there are 20 sts on needle #1, 40 sts on

needle #2, and 20 sts on needle #3, and so that the "seam line" is between needles #1 and #3.

DIVIDE FOR HEEL

Knit across the first 19 sts on needle #1 with needle #3, sl1 wyf. There are 40 sts on the heel needle and 40 sts on needle #2 to be held for instep. Turn work.

Row 1: K1 tbl, p38, sl1 wyf. Turn.
Row 2: K1 tbl, k38, sl1 wyf. Turn.

Repeat these last two rows 11 more times for a total of 12 repeats. End with Row 1 ready to begin a RS row (24 rows total).

Row 1: K1 tbl, k14, k2 tog, k6, SSK, k14, sl1 wyf.
Row 2 and all even rows: K1 tbl, purl to last st, sl1 wyf.
Row 3: K1 tbl, k13, k2 tog, k6, SSK, k13, sl1 wyf.

Row 5: K1 tbl, k12, k2 tog, k6, SSK, k12, sl1 wyf.

Row 7: K1 tbl, k11, k2 tog, k6, SSK, k11, sl1 wyf.

End ready to begin a RS row. There are 32 heel sts.

TURN HEEL

K1 tbl, k18, SSK, turn. Sl1, p6, p2 tog, turn.

*Sl1, k6, SSK, turn. Sl1, p6, p2 tog, turn. Repeat from * until all sts are worked. End ready to begin a RS row. There are 8 heel sts.

GUSSETS

Knit across 8 heel sts, pick up and k16 sts along right side of heel flap. With an empty needle, work across the instep sts. With an empty needle, pick up and k16 sts along left side of heel flap; then knit the first 4 sts from the heel needle onto this last needle. There are 20 sts on needle #1, 40 instep sts on needle #2, and 20 sts on needle #3. Divide the instep sts onto two needles.

Work even until foot length measures 2½ inches less than desired finished length.

SHAPE TOE

Round 1: *K6, K2 tog; repeat from * around.

Rounds 2-7: Work even.

Round 8: *K5, K2 tog; repeat from * around.

Rounds 9-13: Work even.

Round 14: *K4, K2 tog; repeat from * around.

Rounds 15-18: Work even.

Continue in this manner working one less stitch and one less plain round between each decrease round until you work one plain round only. K2 tog all around. Break yarn leaving a 10-inch tail. Thread a blunt-point needle. Draw it through the remaining sts. Tighten up to finish the toe.

Weave in ends. Block socks under a damp towel or on sock blockers.

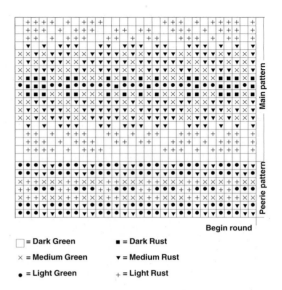

☐ = Dark Green	■ = Dark Rust	
× = Medium Green	▼ = Medium Rust	
● = Light Green	+ = Light Rust	

These boldly striped socks were inspired by the description of stockings knit on the island of Guernsey in a time when stocking knitting was an important part of life. The heel has a Balbriggan Heel shaping and the toe is shaped with the Wide Toe Version #1.

Materials: Brown Sheep Company's Wildfoote (75% washable wool, 25% Nylon, 50g/approx. 215 yards) #Sy-10 Plain Vanilla, #Sy-05 Black Orchid, and #SY-01 Licorice Stick, 1 skein each color.

Set of four #0 double-point needles or size to give gauge.

Gauge: 18 sts and 24 rows = 2 inches over Stockinette stitch worked in the round.

Note: When working striped pattern, do not break off the colors after each use. Carry them along the "seam line", being careful to catch them in. Leave enough slack in the carried yarn so it doesn't pull.

LEG

CO 80 sts with Plain Vanilla over the index finger and Black Orchid over the thumb using the Continental method. Make a loop using both colors. (Loop doesn't figure in the total stitch count.) When all sts have been cast on, remove the loop made up of the two colors. Divide the sts evenly onto 3 needles. Join into a round being careful not to twist sts. This join marks the "seam line" and beginning of the round.

Braid Pattern

Round 1: *K1 Plain Vanilla, k1 Black Orchid; repeat from * around.

Round 2: Bring both colors to the front of the work. Keep them in the same order as on previous round. *P1 Plain Vanilla, p1 Black Orchid, always bringing the next color to be used OVER the top of the last color used. Repeat from * around.

Round 3: *P1 Plain Vanilla, p1 Black Orchid, always bringing the next color to be used UNDER the last color used. Repeat from * around.

Repeat these three rounds one more time.
Bring both colors to the back.
K2 rounds with Plain Vanilla.
Continue with Striped Pattern (10 round repeat) as follows:
3 rounds Black Orchid, 1 round Plain Vanilla, 5 rounds Licorice Stick, 1 round Plain Vanilla. Repeat these 10 rounds 6 more times for a total of 7 repeats. K3 rounds Black Orchid and 1 round Plain Vanilla. Break off yarns, leaving an 8-inch tail.

DIVIDE FOR HEEL

Slip first 20 sts, as to purl, from needle #1 onto needle #3 and place the remaining 40 sts onto another needle to be held for instep.

Row 1: With right side facing, attach Licorice Stick. K40 heel sts. Turn.

Row 2: Sl1, p39 sts. Turn.

Row 3: Sl1, k39 sts. Turn.

Repeat these last 2 rows until you have 36 heel rows total. End with Row 2 ready to begin a RS row.

TURN HEEL

Row 1: Sl1, k7, k2 tog, k8, k2 tog, (SSK, k8) twice.

Row 2 and all even rows: Sl1, purl remaining sts.

Row 3: Sl1, k7, k2 tog, k6, k2 tog, SSK, k6, SSK, k8.

Row 5: Sl1, k7, k2 tog, k4, k2 tog, SSK, k4, SSK, k8.

Row 7: Sl1, k7, k2 tog, k2, k2 tog, SSK, k2, SSK, k8.

Row 9: Sl1, k7, (k2 tog) twice, (SSK) twice, k8.

Row 10: Same as Row 2.

There are 20 heel sts. Divide these 20 sts in half onto two needles. Break yarn leaving a 12-inch tail. Kitchener Stitch the two sets of 10 sts together.

FOOT

Using Licorice Stick, and beginning at the place under the heel at the Kitchener stitch join, pick up and k23 sts along right side of heel flap. With an empty needle, knit across the instep sts. With an empty needle, pick up and k23 sts along left side of heel. There are 23 sts each on needles #1 and #3, and 40 instep sts on needle #2.

SHAPE GUSSETS

Round 1: Work even in established striped pattern.

Round 2: Work to 3 sts from end of needle #1; k2 tog, k1. Knit across needle #2 in established pattern. K1, SSK at the beginning of needle #3. Knit to end of round.

Rounds 3 & 4: Work even in established pattern.

Repeat these last 3 rounds until there are 20 sts each on needles #1 and #3, and 40 sts on needle #2. 80 sts total.

Continue in established pattern until foot measures $2\frac{1}{2}$ inches less than desired finished length. End having worked 3 rounds with Black Orchid and 1 with Plain Vanilla. Break off Plain Vanilla and Black Orchid. Work toe shaping with Licorice Stick.

SHAPE TOE

Round 1: Knit to 4 sts from the end of needle #1; k2 tog, k2. K2, SSK at the beginning of needle #2; knit to last 4 sts from the end of needle #2; k2 tog, k2. K2, SSK at the beginning of needle #3. Knit to end of round.

Round 2: Work even.

Repeat these two rounds until there are 10 sts each on needles #1 and #3, and 20 sts on needle #2. Now work Round 1 (the decrease round) only until there are 3 sts each on needles #1 and #3, and 6 sts on needle #2. Knit across the sts on needle #1 with needle #3. This places the 6 back sts together onto one needle. Break yarn, leaving a 10-inch tail. Kitchener stitch the two sets of 6 sts together.

Weave in ends. Block socks under a damp towel or on sock blockers.

It seems earthy, practical socks are always designed with men in mind—as if women never herded sheep or worked in the fields or went on a hike! These socks, adapted from a pair from the Shetland Island of Foula, are women's socks. They will make good boot or Birkenstock socks. Their design, like the Welsh Coun-

try Stockings, reflects the use of natural colored wool in the welt ribbing, the heel, and the toe. The heel is reinforced with slipped stitches and is shaped with a Round Heel. A Star Toe completes the foot.

Materials: Brown Sheep Company's Nature Spun 3 ply sport (100% wool, 100g/approx. 368 yards) #730 Natural, #880 Charcoal, 1 skein each.

Set of 5 #1 double-point needles or size to give gauge.

Gauge: 18 sts and 22 rounds = 2 inches over ribbed pattern worked in the round, unstretched and before blocking.

LEG

CO 72 sts with Natural using the Continental method. Divide the sts evenly onto 3 needles (knit with needle #4—needle #5 will be used for the toe). Join into a round being careful not to twist sts. This join marks the "seam line" and beginning of the round.

Welt ribbing:

Round 1: P2, * k2, p1, k2, p3. Repeat from * ending k2, p1, k2, p1. Continue in ribbing as established for 19 rounds total. Break off Natural. Join Charcoal and begin ribbed leg pattern:

Round 1: K1, p1, * k5, p1, k1, p1. Repeat from * ending k5, p1.

Round 2: Work as Round 1.

Round 3: P2, * k5, p3. Repeat from * ending k5, p1.

Round 4: Work as Round 3.

Repeat these 4 rounds for leg pattern.

SHAPE CALF

On the 11th round of the leg pattern, decrease as follows: P1, SSP; work in established pattern to last 2 sts; end p2 tog.

Keeping to established pattern, repeat these decreases every 8th round 3 more times for a total of 4 repeats. After the last decrease round, work Round 4, then Rounds 1 and 2 over the seam sts. The pattern will now be k3, *p3, k5, repeat from * ending k2. Work to end of round. 64 sts remain.

Continue even on these sts in established pattern until leg measures approximately 8 inches or desired length to top of heel.

Adjust the sts so that there are 17 sts on needle #1, 31 sts on needle #2, and 16 sts on needle #3, and so that the "seam line" is between needles #1 and #3.

DIVIDE FOR HEEL

Knit across the 17 sts on needle #1 with needle #3. There are 33 sts on the heel needle and 31 sts on needle #2 to be held for instep. Turn the work.

Row 1: Sl1, p32. Turn.

Row 2: Sl1, *sl1, k1. Repeat from * across row. Turn.

Row 3: Sl1, p 32. Turn.

Repeat these last two rows 15 more times for a total of 16 repeats. End with Row 2. Break off Charcoal. Join Natural. Purl the last row omitting the sl1 at the beginning of the row.

TURN HEEL

K19, SSK, k1, turn. Sl1, p6, p2 tog, p1, turn.

*Sl1, knit to within one stitch of the gap, SSK, k1, turn. Sl1, purl to within one stitch of the gap, p2 tog, p1. Repeat from * until all sts are worked. End ready to begin a RS row. There are 19 heel sts. With Natural, sl1, k8. You are now at the center of the heel. Break off Natural. Join Charcoal and k10.

GUSSETS

Pick up and k16 sts along right side of the heel flap. With an empty needle, work across the instep sts in established pattern. With an empty needle, pick up and k16 sts along left side of heel flap; then knit the first 9 sts from the heel needle onto this last needle. There are 26 sts on needle #1, 31 sts on needle #2, and 25 sts on needle #3.

SHAPE GUSSETS

Round 1: Work even in Stockinette stitch and pattern across instep sts.

Round 2: Work to 3 sts away from the end of needle #1, k2 tog, k1. Work across instep sts in established pattern. K1, SSK at the beginning of needle #3. Knit to end of round.

Rounds 3 & 4: Work even, keeping instep sts in established pattern.

Repeat the last three rounds until you have 17 sts on needle #1, 31 sts on needle #2, and 16 sts on needle #3. Continue even in established pattern until foot length measures 2 inches less than desired length. End with Round 4 of ribbing pattern. Break off Charcoal. Join Natural.

SHAPE TOE

Place the last st on needle #1 onto needle #2 and divide the sts on needle #2 onto two needles. You should have 16 sts on each needle.

Round 1: K2 tog at the end of every needle.

Round 2: Work even.

Repeat these 2 rounds 5 more times for a total of 6 repeats. Now work Round 1 (the decrease round) only until there are 2 sts on each needle. Break off the yarn leaving a 10-inch tail. Thread a blunt-point needle and draw it through the remaining sts. Tighten up to finish the toe.

Weave in all ends. Block socks under a damp towel or on sock blockers.

The Royal Ontario Museum in Toronto, Canada, has a small collection of Ukrainian socks, one of which offered the inspiration for this design. All the socks in the museum are colorful and the designs are of patterns set in striped backgrounds. These socks are shaped like those found in Turkey, the Balkans, and throughout the Middle East. They start either at the toe or at the top and are worked to the opposite end with the heel added in last. The socks in this design are worked from the top down to the toe and then the heel is added. The Peasant Heel is similar to the Wedge Toe shaping. These socks are sized for a woman.

Materials: Renaissance Yarns' Froehlich-Wolle Sedrun (90% wool, 10% nylon, 50g/approx. 131 yards) #5558 Parchment, #5334 Wine, #5588 Blue, #5562 Gold, and #5581 Brown, 1 skein each color.

Set of five #3 double-point needles or size to give gauge.

One yard of waste yarn.

Gauge: 14 sts and 16 rounds = 2 inches over pattern worked in the round.

RIGHT SOCK

LEG

CO 56 sts with Parchment over the index finger and Brown over the thumb using the Continental method. Make a loop using both colors. (Loop doesn't figure in the total stitch count.) When all sts have been cast on, remove the loop made up of the two colors. Divide the sts evenly onto 3 needles (knit with needle #4—needle #5 will be used for the heel). Join into a round being careful not to twist sts. This join marks the "seam line" and beginning of the round.

Round 1: *P1 with Parchment, p1 with Brown, repeat from * bringing the Parchment UNDER the Brown each time and the Brown OVER the Parchment.

Work 44 rows of Graph A changing colors as indicated on chart.

Heel preparation round:

With waste yarn, k28 sts. Break off waste yarn. Slide sts back to the beginning of the round (where the waste yarn begins). Work 41 rounds of Graph B changing colors as indicated on chart.

SHAPE TOE

Round 1: Knit 1 rnd Blue. [K1, SSK, work Toe Graph to last 3 sts, k2 tog, k1] 2 times.

Round 2: Work even following graph.

Repeat these 2 rounds 5 more times for a total of 12 rounds. Then decrease every round 5 times keeping pattern as established. There are 3 sts each on needles #1 and #3, and 6 sts on needle #2. Knit across the sts on needle #1 with needle #3. This places the 6 back sts together onto one needle. Break yarn leaving a 10-inch tail. Kitchener stitch the 2 sets of 6 sts together to finish the toe.

SHAPE HEEL

Carefully pull out the waste yarn knit into half the sts at the point between Graph A and Graph B. There are 28 live sts on one edge and 27 live sts on the other edge. Place these sts on 4 needles, starting at the side where the seam runs down the leg and working around the opening. There are 14 sts on 3 needles and 13 sts on the 4th needle.

With an empty needle and Blue, pick up and k1 new stitch tbl, k14 sts. With an empty needle, knit across the next 14 sts. With an empty needle, pick up and k1 new stitch tbl and knit across the next 14 sts. With an empty needle, knit across the last 13 sts, pick up and k1 new stitch tbl. There are 15 sts on needle #1, 14 sts on needle #2, 15 sts on needle #3, and 14 sts on needle #4.

K8 rounds.

Round 1: [K1, SSK, k12. K11, k2 tog, k1] 2 times.

Repeat this last round 10 more times for a total of 11 repeats (44 sts decreased). There are 14 sts remaining (4 sts on needle #1, 3 sts on needle #2, 4 sts on needle #3, and 3 sts on needle #4). Knit across the sts on needle #2 with needle #1. Knit across the sts on needle #4 with needle #3. Break yarn leaving a 10-inch tail. Kitchener stitch the 2 sets of 7 sts together to finish the heel.

Sock from Crimea, Ukraine.

LEFT SOCK

Work as for right sock but place seam so that it runs down right side of leg.

Heel preparation: Complete Graph A. Slip the last 28 sts of the round backwards. Knit a waste yarn into these last 28 sts. Continue following Graph B as for right sock.

Weave in ends. Block socks under a damp towel or on sock blockers.

Graph A **Graph B**

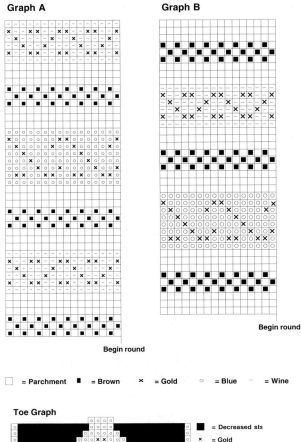

Begin round

☐ = Parchment ■ = Brown ✕ = Gold ○ = Blue – = Wine

Toe Graph

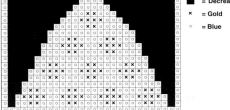

■ = Decreased sts

✕ = Gold

○ = Blue

Flammegarn is the Norwegian name for yarn dyed by wrapping rush, twine, or other material tightly around the skeined yarn and placing it in a dye bath. When the yarn is dry, the rush is removed and the yarn has a mottled effect, rather than being one solid color. This type of "tie-dyed" yarn is not unique to Nor-way, but is used for stockings and other textiles throughout Scandinavia, Britain, and elsewhere. The Flammegarn Socks have a Shaped Common Heel, and a Wide Toe (Version #2). These socks are sized for a man.

Materials: Renaissance Yarns' Froehlich-Wolle Special Multicolor (80% wool, 20% nylon, 50g/approx. 225 yards) #7288 Indigo, 3 skeins (includes reinforcing yarn).

Set of four #1 double-point needles or size to give gauge.

Gauge: 16 sts and 24 rounds = 2 inches over pattern worked in the round.

LEG

CO 70 sts using the Continental method. Divide the sts as follows: 19 sts on needle #1, 32 sts on needle #2, and 19 sts on needle #3. Join into a round being careful not to twist sts. This join marks the "seam line" and beginning of the round.

P1, k3 sts using both ends of the yarn. Drop the CO tail. *P2, k3; repeat from *, ending p1. Continue in ribbing as established until work measures 3½ inches. On last round of rib increase 1 st between last and first purl sts. This is the "seam" stitch and it will now be the beginning of the round.

Round 1: P1 ("seam" stitch), k2, sl1 as to purl, *k4, sl1; repeat from *, ending k2.

Round 2: P1, knit to end of round.

Repeat these 2 rounds for 4 inches.

SHAPE CALF

Round 1: P1, SSK, continue in established pattern until 2 sts from end of round, k2 tog.

Repeat this decrease round every 8th round 3 times total (6 sts decreased). Work to end of round. 65 sts remain.

Continue even on these sts in established pattern until sock measures 11 inches total or desired length to top of heel. There should be 17 sts on needle #1, 32 sts on needle #2, and 16 sts on needle #3, and the "seam line" should be between needles #1 and #3. Beginning at seam, join reinforcing yarn.

DIVIDE FOR HEEL

Knit across the first 16 sts on needle #1 with needle #3, sl1 wyf. There are 33 sts on the heel needle and 32 sts on needle #2 to be held for instep. The "seam" stitch will be in the center of the heel needle. Turn the work.

Row 1: K1 tbl, p15, k1 ("seam" stitch), p15, sl1 wyf. Turn.

Row 2: K1 tbl, knit to center st, p1, knit to last st, sl1 wyf. Turn.

Repeat these 2 rows 15 more times for a total of 16 repeats. End with Row 1 ready to begin a RS row.

TURN HEEL

Row 1: K1 tbl, work to 2 sts before the "seam" stitch, k2 tog, p1 ("seam" stitch), SSK, work to 1 st before end of row, sl1 wyf. Turn.

Row 2: K1 tbl, p to center st, k1, p to last st, sl1 wyf.

Repeat these 2 rows 4 more times for a total of 5 repeats. On the last row of the heel, purl the "seam" stitch together with the stitch before it and purl the last st (instead of sl1 wyf). There are 22 heel sts.

Break both yarns leaving a 10-inch tail. Cut reinforcing yarn. Divide these 22 sts equally onto 2 needles. Kitchener stitch the two sets of 11 sts together.

GUSSETS

Beginning at center back of heel flap (at the Kitchener stitch join), pick up and k21 sts tbl along the right side of the heel flap. With an empty needle, pick up and k1 st tbl at the beginning of the instep sts; work across the instep sts in established pattern; pick up and k1 tbl at the end of the instep sts. With an empty needle, pick up and knit 21 sts tbl along the left side of the heel flap ending at center back of heel. There are 21 sts on needle #1, 34 sts on needle #2, and 21 sts on needle #3.

SHAPE GUSSETS

Round 1: Work to 3 sts away from the end of needle #1; k2 tog, k1. SSK at the beginning of needle #2; work across instep sts in established pattern to last 2 sts; k2 tog. K1, SSK at the beginning of needle #3. Work to end of round.

Rounds 2 & 3: Work even in established pattern.

Repeat these 3 rounds (but omit the decreases on the instep needle) 4 more times for a total of 5 repeats. There are 16 sts each on needles #1 and #3, and 32 instep sts on needle #2. Continue even in established pattern on these 64 sts until foot length measures 2½ inches less than desired length. Discontinue pattern. Join reinforcing yarn.

SHAPE TOE

Round 1: Knit to 6 sts away from the end of needle #1, k2 tog, k4. K4, SSK at the beginning of needle #2; knit to 6 sts away from end of needle #2, k2 tog, k4. K4, SSK at the beginning of needle #3. Knit to end of round.

Rounds 2, 3 & 4: Work even.

Round 5: Repeat Round 1.

Rounds 6 & 7: Work even.

Round 8: Repeat Round 1.

Round 9: Work even.

Repeat the last 2 rounds until there are 5 sts each on needles #1 and #3, and 10 sts on needle #2.

Knit across the 5 sts on needle #1 with needle #3; this places the 10 back sts together onto one needle. Break both yarns leaving a 10-inch tail. Kitchener stitch the 2 sets of 10 sts together to finish the toe.

Weave in ends. Block socks under a damp towel or on sock blockers.

BIBLIOGRAPHY

Andresen, Gudren; Green, Lisbeth; and Nødskov, Gitte. *Bondestrik: strømper til Maend og Kvinder*. Horsens, Denmark: Danske Folkedansere, 1983.

Ashelford, Jane. *A Visual History of Costume: The Sixteenth Century*. London: Batsford, 1983.

Balneaves, Elizabeth. *The Windswept Isles*. London: John Gifford, 1977.

Barnes, Ishbel C. "The Aberdeen Stocking Trade". *Textile History* Vol. VIII, 1977.

Beckmann, John. *A History of Inventions, Discoveries, and Origins, Vol. II*. Translated by William Johnston. 1846. Reprint. Amsterdam: B.M. Israel, 1974.

Bellinger, L., Pfister, R. "The Excavation at Dura Europos. Final Report IV, The Textiles". New Haven, Connecticut: Yale University Press, 1945.

Bennett, Helen. *Scottish Knitting*. Aylesbury, Bucks, England: Shire Publications, 1986.

Birley, Robin. *The Roman Documents from Vindolanda*. Carvoran, Greenland, Northumberland: Roman Army Museum Publications, 1990.

Bossert, Helmuth Th. *Folk Art of Europe*. New York: Hastings House, 1976.

———. *Peasant Art of Europe and Asia*. New York: Praeger, 1966.

Burnam, Dorothy. "Coptic Knitting: An Ancient Technique". *Textile History* Vol XIII, 1972.

Crowfoot, Elisabeth; Pritchard, Frances; and Staniland, Kay. *Textiles and Clothing c.1150–c.1450*. London: HMSO, 1992.

Cumming, Valerie. *A Visual History of Costume: The Seventeenth Century*. London: Batsford, 1984.

Cunnington, Phillis. *Costume in Pictures*. Rev. ed. London: The Herbert Press, 1981.

Davenport, Millia. *The Book of Costume, vols. I and II*. New York: Crown, 1948.

Ekstrand, Gudrun. "Some Early Silk Textiles in Sweden". *Textile History* Vol. XIII (2), 1982.

Emery, Irene. *The Primary Structure of Fabrics*. Washington, D.C.: The Textile Museum, 1966.

Farrell, Jeremy. *Socks and Stockings*. London: B.T. Batsford, 1992.

Fatelewitz, Madelynn. "Knitting in the North Atlantic: Sheep and Wool Shape Faeroe Island Culture". In *Threads Magazine* (April/May 1988): 51-55.

Frazer, R.M. *Poems of Hesiod*. Norman, Oklahoma: University of Oklahoma Press, 1983.

Gerrers, Veronika. *The Influence of Ottoman Turkish Textiles and Costume in Eastern Europe*. Monograph 4. Toronto: Royal Ontario Museum, 1982.

Grant, William, and Murison, David D. eds. *Scottish National Dictionary*. Vol. VIII. Edinburgh, Scotland, 1971.

Grass, Anna, and Grass, Milton. *Stockings for a Queen: The Life of the Rev. William Lee, the Elizabethan Inventor*. Cranbury, New Jersey: A.S. Barnes & Co., 1969.

Grass, Milton. *The History of Hosiery*. New York: Fairchild Publications, Inc., 1955.

Hald, Margrethe. "Ancient Textile Techniques in Egypt and Scandinavia: A Comparative Study by Margrethe Hald". In *Acta Archaeologica, Vol. XVII*. Copenhagen: Ejnar Munksgaard, 1945.

Harte, N.B., and Ponting, K.G. "Textile History and Economic History: Essays in Honour of Miss Julia de Lacy Mann". In *The Fantastical Folly of Fashion: the English Stocking Knitting Industry, 1500–1700* by Joan Thirsk. Manchester University Press, 1973.

Harrison, William. *The Description of England*. 1587. Edited by Georges Eldelen. Reprint. Ithaca, New York: Cornell University Press, 1968.

Kelly, Francis M., and Schwabe, Randolph. *Historic Costume*. New York: Charles Scribner's Sons, 1925.

Kjellberg, Anne; Gravjord, Ingebjorg; Gerd, Aarsland Rosander; and Svendsen, Anne-Lise. *Strikking i Norge*. Norges Husflidslag. Otta, Norway: Landsbruksforlaget, 1987.

Konsin, K. *Slimkoeesemed*. Estonia: Kirjastus Kunst Tallinn, 1972.

Laver, James, ed. *Costumes of the Western World (Fashions of the Renaissance in England, France, Spain and Holland)*. New York: Harper and Brothers, 1951.

Lester, Katherine Morris, and Oerke, Bess Viola. *Accessories of Dress*. Peoria, Ill.: The Manual Arts Press, 1940.

Lewis C.T., and Short C. *Latin Dictionary*. 1897. Reprint. Oxford: Clarendon Press, 1962.

McClintock, H.F. *Old Irish and Highland Dress*. Dundalk, Ireland: Dundalgan Press (W. Tempest), 1950.

McGregor, Sheila. *The Complete Book of Traditional Fair Isle Knitting*. London: B.T. Batsford, 1981.

Nicoll, Maud Churchill. *How To Knit Socks*. Cambridge, Massachusetts: University Press, 1915.

———. *Knitting and Sewing*. New York: George H. Doran, 1918.

Nicolson, James R. *Traditional Life in Shetland*. London: Robert Hale, 1978.

Nordland, Odd. *Primitive Scandinavian Textiles in Knotless Netting*. Oslo, Norway: Oslo University Press, 1961.

Nylén, Anna-Maja. *Swedish Handcraft*. Lund, Sweden: Hekan Ohlssons Förlag, 1976.

Owen, Trefor M. *The Customs and Traditions of Wales*. Cardiff: University of Wales Press, 1991.

Pagoldh, Susanne. *Nordic Knitting*. Loveland, Colorado: Interweave Press, 1991.

Oxford English Dictionary. Vol. XV, XV1. 2nd ed. Oxford: Clarendon Press, 1989.

Oxford Latin Dictionary. Oxford: Clarendon Press, 1982.

Peacock, John. *Costume 1066-1966*. London: Thames and Hudson, 1986.

Petrie, W.M. Flinders. *Hawara, Biahmu, and Arsinoe*. London: Field and Tuer, 1889.

Ränk, Gustav. *Old Estonia, The People and Culture*. Uralic and Altaic Series, vol. 112. Bloomington, Ind.: Indiana Univerrsity Press, 1976.

Rutt, Richard. *History of Handknitting*. Loveland, Colorado: Interweave Press, 1987.

Ryder, H.P. *Cycling and Shooting Knickerbocker Stockings*. New York, Macmillan and Co., 1896.

Schildhauer, Johannes. *The Hansa: History and Culture*. Edition Leipzig, 1985.

Sedgewick, Adam. *Adam Sedgewick's Dent: a facsimile reprint in one volume of two classics of Dales history*. A Memorial by the Trustees of Cowgill Chapel (1868) and Supplement to the Memorial (1870). With introduction and notes by David Boulton. Privately published by R.F.G. Hollett and Son, Sedberg, and David Boulton, Dent, 1984.

Sichel, Marion. *Costume Reference 1: Roman Britain and the Middle Ages*. London: Batsford, 1977.

———. *Costume Reference 2: Tudors and Elizabethans*. London: Batsford, 1977.

———. *Costume Reference 3: Jacobean, Stuart and Restoration*. London: Batsford, 1977.

Souden, David. *The Victorian Village*. London: Collins and Brown, 1991.

Skarhaug, Kjersti, and Vanberg, Bent. *Norwegian Bunads*. Oslo, Norway: Hjemmenes Forlag, 1982.

Squire, Geoffrey. *Dress and Society 1560–1970*. New York: Viking Press, 1974.

Stavridi, Margaret. *History of Costume*. Boston: Plays Inc., 1970.

Stewart, Janice S. *The Folk Art of Norway*. 1953. Reprint. New York: Dover Publishers, 1972.

Tedre, Ülo. *Estonian Customs and Traditions*. Tallinn, Estonia: Tallinn Perioodika, 1985.

Thomas, Mary. *Mary Thomas's Knitting Book*. New York: Dover Publications, 1972.

Tibbott, Minwel. "Knitting Stockings in Wales—A Domestic Craft". *Folklife Studies*. Cardiff, Wales, 1978.

Turnau, Irene. "The Diffusion of Knitting in Medieval Europe." In *Cloth and Clothing in Medieval Europe*. Essays in memory of professor E.M. Carus-Wilson. London: Heinemann Educational Books, 1983.

———. *History of Dress in Central and Eastern Europe from the Sixteenth to the Eighteenth Centuries*. Warsaw, Poland: Polish Academy of Sciences, 1991.

———. *History of Knitting Before Mass Production*. Translated by Agneizka Szonert. Warszawa, Poland: Oficyna Wydawnicza, 1991.

———. "Stockings from the Coffins of the Pomeranian Princes Preserved in the National Museum in Szczecin." *Textile History* Vol. VIII, 1977.

Upitis, Lizbeth. *Latvian Mittens: Traditional Designs and Techniques*. St. Paul, Minn.: Dos Tejedoras, 1981.

Watterson, Barbara. *Coptic Egypt*. Edinburgh: Scottish Academic Press, 1988.

Wild, John Peter. *Textiles in Archaeology*. Aylesbury, Bucks, England: Shire Publications, 1988.

Wilton, Mary Margaret. *The Book of Costume*. 1846. Reprint. Lopez Island, Wash.: R.L. Shep, 1986.

INDEX

YARN SUPPLIERS

Berroco, Inc., PO Box 367, Uxbridge, Massachusetts 01569. (800) 343-4948. *Wendy Guernsey*

Brown Sheep Company, The, 100662 Country Road 16, Mitchell, Nebraska 69357. (308) 635-2198. (800) 826-9136. *Wildfoote and Nature Spun 3 Ply*

Dale of Norway, N16W23390 Stoneridge Dr., Ste. A, Waukesha, Wisconsin 53188. (414) 544-1996. (800) 441-3253. *Heilo*

Jamieson and Smith, 90 North Road, Lerwick, Shetland Islands, ZE1 0PQ Scotland. *2 Ply Shetland Jumperweight*

Nordic Fiber Arts, Four Cutts Road, Durham, New Hampshire 03824. (603) 868-1196. *Finullgarn*

Wheelsmith Wools, PO Box 13, Centre Hall, PA 16828. *Shetland Jumperweight*

2 Ply Shetland Jumperweight and Satakieli are is available retail from:

Schoolhouse Press, 6899 Carry Bluff, Pittsville, Wisconsin 54466. (715) 884-2799.

The Wooly West, PO Box 58306, Salt Lake City, Utah 84158. (888) 487-9665.